Also available at all good book stores

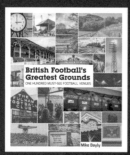

9781785316470

9781785313929

9781785315466

9781785315688

9781785315275

9781785315091

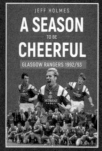

9781785313257

9781785312304

9781908051332

RANGERS

MINUTE BY MINUTE

RANGERS
MINUTE
BY MINUTE

Covering More Than 500 Goals,
Penalties, Red Cards and
Other Intriguing Facts

DAVID JACKSON

First published by Pitch Publishing, 2021

Pitch Publishing
A2 Yeoman Gate
Yeoman Way
Worthing
Sussex
BN13 3QZ
www.pitchpublishing.co.uk
info@pitchpublishing.co.uk

ISBN 978 1 78531 847 4

Typesetting and origination by Pitch Publishing
Printed and bound in India by Replika Press Pvt. Ltd

Contents

Dedicated to the memory of Davie Cooper.

And to Jimmy Parlane, former Rangers player and proud father of the King of Ibrox, Derek Parlane.

Acknowledgements

Rangers: Minute by Minute was a hard yet hugely enjoyable book to write and research, but thanks to certain resource outlets, it was made a lot easier.

Trying to get every moment in the Light Blues' history that really mattered and then discovering the minute it was scored or happened in – before describing it in detail – takes a long time and many, many hours, but hopefully you'll enjoy the end result and all the hard work will have been well worth the while. And if it brings back some happy memories along the way, so much the better.

The goal times, dismissals and key incidents are taken from various resources, cross-checked, and checked again, but some of the older timings may differ as the minutes in question weren't quite as accurately recorded by journalists and historians way back when – but that comes with the territory.

That said, BBC Scotland match reports, Sky Sports games, endless YouTube highlights, countless newspaper clippings and old match reports that sometimes tested my eyesight to the limit, plus the official Rangers website and various other fan sites and stats platforms such as Opta, Soccerbase, Transfermarkt and 11v11 all proved extremely helpful. The legendary Gers message board Follow Follow was incredibly helpful in helping me get the man who wrote the foreword to this book as well, so a massive thanks, guys.

Each minute, from the earliest record of an incident – with several in the first few seconds – to the dying embers of matches in extra time and penalties is logged in the pages that follow, though it's inevitable there will be one or two glaring omissions. If anything jumps out, be sure to tell me via the publisher so I can add it to future editions.

And as an added bonus, there is every goal scored during the magnificent 2020/21 campaign as Rangers finally reclaimed the Scottish Premiership crown – an unbeaten league campaign doesn't happen very often, does it? It just seemed an obvious thing to include.

And I'll be up front with you, too. I live south of the border and support an English team, but Rangers have always been my Scottish team from being a lad and my 'second club'.

In other matters, I'd like to also thank Paul and Jane Camillin – the tireless siblings who mastermind Pitch Publishing – for green-lighting this series of *Minute by Minute* books.

To be able to finally write about this fantastic football club was a genuine pleasure and I hope that shines through in the pages that follow. Having a *Rangers: Minute by Minute* was a no-brainer and, finally, we have an end result.

Last, but by no means least, a massive thank you to Rangers legend Derek Parlane for providing the wonderful foreword to this book. What a genuinely lovely guy he was to talk to and I can't think of anyone better to introduce this book.

Anyway, enough from me – on with the show.

Introduction

Glasgow Rangers Football Club have an extraordinary history and *Rangers: Minute by Minute* takes you through the Light Blues' matchday history and records the historic goals, incidents and memorable moments, and the minutes they happened in.

The book covers from Rangers' early beginnings and successes to the days of domestic domination and the early days of William Wilton, to the glorious Bill Struth era and on to the many successes enjoyed under the tutelage of Jock Wallace and up to the present era with Steven Gerrard – as time goes on, it will be somebody else in the hot seat because football never stays still and is constantly evolving.

Learn about the club's most historic events or simply relive some truly unforgettable moments from the Gers' history, from the first games on record to the title-winning campaign of 2020/21.

Included are all the Scottish Premier League successes, the Scottish Cup, Scottish League Cup triumphs and, of course, the many memorable European nights at Ibrox and beyond over the years – not forgetting the moments when doubles and treble triumphs were sealed.

And of course, what book on Rangers would be complete without the many goals scored against Celtic in the hundreds of Old Firm battles down the years?

And it would be remiss of the author not to include the events of Helicopter Sunday and all the drama and quite incredible turnaround of events (including the helicopter pilot of course) of that particular day.

You will also discover just how many times a crucial goal has been scored at the same minute so often over the years. From those scored in the opening few seconds to the last-gasp extra-time winners, added to the drama of numerous penalty shoot-outs they have thrilled generations of Rangers fans around the world.

Included are countless goals from Ally McCoist, Jim Baxter, Colin Stein, Jim Forrest, Derek Parlane, Brian Laudrup, Davie Cooper, John Greig, Gazza, Mark Hateley, Kris Boyd, Kyle Lafferty and right up to the present with the likes of Ryan Kent, Alfredo Morelos and the right-back phenomenon that is James Tavernier (18 goals in one season from a full-back? Unreal).

All of the above and plenty more are featured – a cast of hundreds, in fact, who have played for the Light Blues over the years – plus many players who may not have hit the headlines, but still have played their part in the history of this magnificent club.

Whether it be European glory, an Old Firm clash at Hampden Park or a Challenge Cup Final against Peterhead – plus a Scottish Cup tie against Forres Mechanics – each minute will revive a new memory because it is a fact that Rangers have experienced every possible emotion that Scottish football can throw at them, plus a few more. Now you can discover just when those historic, brilliant, dramatic, or occasionally seemingly run-of-the-mill goals were scored and how they were created as well as a few moments to forget.

Recall, re-live and enjoy them all over again.

Foreword
by Derek Parlane

When I was asked by the author of this book if I could clearly remember the first goal I scored for Rangers and the minute I did it in, it was one of the easiest questions I could ever answer.

Remember it? That's a massive understatement because everything about that moment is etched in my memory as if it were yesterday. Maybe it would have been different if it had been East Stirling or Forfar – I'll never know – but this goal was special on so many levels as we were playing Bayern Munich in the European Cup Winners' Cup semi-final, second leg at Ibrox.

We had drawn the first leg in Munich 1-1 – despite getting absolutely battered, by the way – and we came back to Glasgow two weeks later for the return game. I had absolutely no idea that I'd be playing that night. I was in the squad, but I'd played only two first-team games a couple of weeks before in league matches and, if truth be told, I didn't think I'd done particularly well in either.

So you can imagine my surprise and delight when I was thrown in for this game. Our captain, John Greig, was injured that night and I'll never forget Jock Wallace reading the team out: Number one Peter McCloy; number two, Sandy Jardine; number three, Willie Mathieson; number four Derek Parlane; I never heard the rest of the team!

My dad was sat in the stand that night when the team was announced over the tannoy system – which wasn't the best back then – and he was with four or five of his mates when my name was read out at number four. He told his pals, 'I think they've made a mistake because they said my Derek is playing.'

I was given a particular job in this match to mark Franz Roth, who was one of Bayern's main midfield playmakers, and stick with him throughout the 90 minutes.

I'll never forget standing in the tunnel and seeing the Germans come out before we walked out. Sepp Maier, one of the best goalkeepers in the world; captain Franz Beckenbauer, one of the greatest defenders of all time; Gerd Müller; half that team would be World Cup winners with West Germany just two years later. And there's me – two games played and just 18 years old in one of Rangers' most important games ever.

There were 80,000 inside Ibrox that night and it was electric. We won a corner at the Broomloan Road End and Willie Johnstone took it. Sepp Maier got a fist on it and punched it out and I remember thinking that if I got a little sprint on, I'd have half a chance of getting on the end of it. So I did, and as it landed I hit it with the foot I usually only used to stand on – my left – and caught it sweetly because it shot up into the goalkeeper's top-right corner and into the roof of the net with 21 minutes on the clock. In that moment my life changed forever, and it's a night I will never forget. The boys couldn't catch me as I was running that fast! It was an amazing game; we won 2-0 and went on to the final where we played Dynamo Moscow in Barcelona and won the European Cup Winners' Cup. I was back on the bench because Greigy was fit again.

I think that was my best goal for Rangers, but there are plenty of others that stick in my memory. By the start of the next season I was a regular in the first team and it culminated with maybe the greatest Scottish Cup Final Glasgow has ever seen, between Rangers and Celtic in our centenary year of 1972/73.

It was 5 May – my 20th birthday – and we beat Celtic at Hampden Park. I equalised Kenny Daglish's goal when I scored on 35 minutes – my 27th of my first full season – so that was a very special goal, too. Tommy Forsyth scored the winner on 60 minutes and we won 3-2 in front of 122,714 spectators. So whenever anyone asks me which Rangers goals would I like to re-live, those two immediately spring to mind for obvious reasons.

My dad, Jimmy Parlane, played for Rangers in the 1940s but only a handful of times before his career was interrupted by the Second World War, and while there have been a few other father and son pairs to have lined up for Rangers, my dad and I are the only ones to have both scored for the club against Celtic, which is a nice stat to have. My dad scored on his debut against Celtic and I got maybe 12 goals against them, so it is something I'm still very proud of.

I wanted to emulate my dad and play for Rangers and follow in his footsteps and I know how proud he was. In fact, the night of the day we beat Celtic in the final in '73, he slept with my winners' medal under his pillow! He was a rock throughout my career and was with me all the way.

As a kid my hero was Colin Stein, who joined Rangers when I was still at school. I thought he was a fantastic centre-forward and he scored a couple of hat-tricks early on after joining so he was an instant crowd favourite. I remember when I joined Rangers, I was training alongside people like Colin, John Greig, Willie Johnstone and Willie Henderson and I was just blown away by it all.

The season after we won the European Cup Winners' Cup, I was called into the manager's office before the new season started. Jock Wallace had a Rangers shirt on his knee as I went in and he told me Colin would be leaving the club soon and he said, 'Have a look at this,' as he threw the shirt over to me. I looked on the back it was the number nine jersey so I said, 'What are you telling me?' He said that he was telling me that he wanted to make that shirt my own that season. So, for Steiny to be my hero and for me to replace him and take his number nine shirt, it was a dream come true. I don't think I've ever told him he was my hero when we meet up every now and then with a few other former players. His head would get too big!

Another fantastic Rangers striker was Jim Forrest, who I've never met in person but was a goal machine at Ibrox. I remember walking towards the ground on a European night under the lights when I was 12 and my dad said, 'Derek, look who is walking down the street ahead of us.' I said, 'Dad, that's Jim Forrest!' Again, I was blown away but that was the closest I ever got to him.

There are plenty of great memories during my time at Ibrox. One was when I scored all four goals in a 4-2 victory against Hearts at Tynecastle – one of my favourite grounds – back in January 1974. There was another time we beat Dunfermline 6-1 and I scored five times, so these are games that jump out at me. Just don't ask me to tell you which minute they were all scored in!

I spent almost ten years as a Rangers player and made 303 appearances, scoring 112 goals before joining Leeds United in March 1980. I was only 26 when I left Ibrox and I still feel I left the club too early, but things were happening out of my control and I didn't get much game time in my last two seasons so it felt right at the time to move on.

I look back fondly on my career and was lucky to play for clubs such as Leeds and Manchester City as well, but Rangers has always been my club and always will be. I still think back to that goal against Bayern Munich and wonder 'what if?' What if I hadn't been at that place at that time and hadn't scored? Would I have gone on to have the career I had? I guess the stars aligned for me at that particular minute.

The Rangers fans used to call me the King of Ibrox Park, which I loved. The reason I was given the title was around Christmas time in my first season when I scored one of the four goals we scored against East Fife and to the tune of 'The First Noel' the fans started to sing 'Parlane, Parlane, born is the King of Ibrox Park!' It always makes me smile when I think about it.

The Rangers fans, who have never been anything but fantastic towards me, remember that because I get so many really lovely messages on Instagram. It's greatly appreciated, believe me.

Enjoy the book and I hope it brings back a lot of happy memories – maybe even one or two of my goals might have made it on to the pages that follow.

Derek Parlane
July 2021

Minute by Minute

And we're under way

12 seconds

1 April 1995

Gordon Durie kicks off the game away to Dundee United at Tannadice and the ball is played to Alan McLaren on the right. McLaren punts a long ball forward that the home defence fails to deal with and Durie races on to it then lobs the onrushing keeper to see his shot just bounce inside the left post.

19 seconds

7 November 2009

Kris Boyd puts Rangers 1-0 up against St Mirren with a goal inside the first minute at Ibrox. When John Fleck's shot is saved the ball ricochets off Nacho Novo to Boyd, who makes no mistake from four yards out.

22 seconds

24 April 1976

Rangers clinch the title away to Dundee United with the only goal of the game coming from Derek Johnstone after just 22 seconds. Gers are crowned champions after the 1-0 win at Tannadice with two matches remaining and end up six points clear of second-placed Celtic thanks largely to 16 wins in the last 21 games.

40 seconds

22 April 1950

Rangers take the lead against East Fife with a move straight from the kick-off. In front of a huge 118,262 fans at Hampden Park, the Gers open the scoring when Eddie Rutherford's cross from the right is superbly headed home by Willie Findlay, who dives in to direct his header into the bottom-left corner to get the Light Blues off to the perfect start in the Scottish Cup Final. The Gers will go on to win 3-0 and secure a 13th success in the competition.

47 seconds

3 September 1983

Ally McCoist puts Rangers 1-0 up at Celtic Park as the Light Blues race out of the blocks in the early season Old Firm clash. McCoist wins a free kick when he is clattered by Roy Aitken and after the ball is played out to the right, a low cross is swept home by McCoist from ten yards with a shot that squirms through the keeper. It is the 21-year-old's first Old Firm goal after joining from Sunderland and is the start of a magnificent career for the Ibrox legend.

15 May 2011

Needing to win to secure the Scottish Premier League championship and give manager Walter Smith the perfect send-off, Rangers know they must beat Kilmarnock on the final day of the 2010/11 campaign. It's the fourth time in five years the title race has gone to the last day and with Celtic hosting mid-table Motherwell, the Gers know any slip-up will almost certainly be punished by the Hoops, who sit one point behind going into the final round of matches. The Gers need a good start, and Kyle Lafferty strikes inside the first minute. With 47 seconds on the clock, Steven Davis puts him clear in the first attack of any note as he heads it into his path and the Northern Ireland international darts between two defenders before deftly chipping goalkeeper Cammy Bell from the edge of the penalty area to make it 1-0 to the Light Blues.

1

16 April 1936

Bob McPhail scores in the first minute of the 1936 Scottish Cup Final against Third Lanark. Few in the near-89,000 Hampden Park crowd imagined that McPhail's strike would be the only goal of the game, but the 1-0 victory over plucky underdogs Lanark gives the Light Blues a third successive Scottish Cup triumph and a tenth success in total.

19 April 1972

Sandy Jardine scores a spectacular and vital goal for Rangers with just one minute on the clock of the European Cup Winners' Cup semi-final, second leg. After a 1-1 first-leg draw away to Bayern Munich, Jardine cuts in from the right before firing a left-footed drive into the top-left corner from 20 yards out to send the 80,000 Ibrox crowd into raptures.

1 September 1993

Mark Hateley keeps his nerve to give the Gers a 1-0 lead against Aberdeen in the Scottish League Cup quarter-final at Ibrox. The linesman had spotted an infringement in the opening seconds so the referee awarded the penalty on his advice and Hateley sends the keeper the wrong way to give the Light Blues the perfect start.

2

30 November 1960

Jim Baxter puts Rangers on the way to a record European victory as he grabs a goal less than two minutes in against German cup winners Borussia Mönchengladbach. Already 3-0 up from the first leg in Germany, Baxter all but seals a place in the semi-finals within the opening moments of the game in front of more than 38,000 Ibrox fans.

19 April 2003

Rangers take an early lead in the Scottish Cup semi-final against Motherwell at Hampden Park. The Light Blues, expected to brush past Well, waste no time as Barry Ferguson, just back from suspension, makes himself space down the left wing before sending an inviting pass to Bert Konterman who drives the ball powerfully past keeper François Dubourdeau to make it 1-0.

24 January 1973

Trailing 3-1 from the first leg of the European Super Cup, Rangers get off to the perfect start in the return game in Amsterdam. A David Smith pass eventually falls for Alex MacDonald who rifles a ferocious shot into the top-left corner to put the Gers 1-0 up on the night and reduce the aggregate arrears to 3-2 in Ajax's favour.

4 November 2000

With just 80 seconds on the clock, St Mirren only half clear Ronald de Boer's corner and the ball falls to Kenny Miller –

making only his third start for Gers – and from just inside the box his lofted shot loops up over a crowd of players including goalkeeper Derek Scrimgour and drops into the net to give the champions a second-minute lead at Ibrox.

26 April 2009

Andrius Velička puts Rangers ahead in the Scottish Cup semi-final at Hampden Park. In the first real attack of the game, Steven Davis brings the ball forward down the right. The Northern Ireland midfielder finds Kris Boyd, whose shot is deflected into the path of Velička and the Lithuanian striker slides in to hit the ball into the roof of net to put Rangers 1-0 up against St Mirren.

10 August 2013

Newly promoted Rangers begin life in Scottish League One in style at home to Brechin City. With more than 44,000 packed into Ibrox for the opening league game of the campaign, the third-tier champions waste no time laying down a marker for the months ahead with a goal inside two minutes. With the club still operating under a transfer ban, former Motherwell player Nicky Law is fielded as a triallist and his low shot deflects across the six-yard box for Chris Hegarty to prod home and start what will be a record-breaking campaign for the Light Blues.

12 March 2014

On the day Rangers can be crowned Scottish League One champions, Lee McCulloch drives home a penalty with just 100 seconds played. As Andy Little heads towards goal, Airdrie keeper Grant Adam rushes out and clumsily brings Little down. The ref decides there is enough cover not to show Adam a red card and McCulloch hands out his own punishment as he drills home the resulting spot-kick to put Gers 1-0 up at Ibrox.

12 May 2019

In the penultimate Scottish Premiership game of the season, Rangers strike early in the latest Old Firm clash at Ibrox. Ryan Kent cuts inside from the left and is brought down on the corner of the Celtic box by Michael Johnston. With a crowded box waiting for a delivery, James Tavernier cleverly sends in a curling free kick that nobody connects with and by the time the keeper realises, the ball has curled into the far corner to give the Gers a 1-0 lead. Incredibly, it is right-back Tavernier's 17th goal of an unforgettable campaign and though the Hoops have already been crowned champions, boss Steven Gerrard know it is vital to lay a marker down for the following season.

3

25 May 2003

On what is effectively a final-day Scottish Premier League title shoot-out with Celtic, Rangers know that a margin of victory of just one goal greater than the Hoops' score at Kilmarnock will bring the championship back to Ibrox. The Gers, hosting Dunfermline Athletic, have to win well and Michael Mols gets his side off to the perfect start. An incisive Rangers move eventually sees the ball at the feet of Claudio Caniggia but his short pass to Mols is slightly behind the Dutch striker, who swivels around and drags a low shot that trundles in off the left-hand post to make it 1-0 and settle Ibrox nerves.

6 February 2011

Ibrox erupts as Jamie Ness scores a stunning goal to put Rangers 1-0 up in the Old Firm Scottish Cup fifth round. El Hadji Diouf's corner is cleared to the edge of the box, where 19-year-old Ness collects the loose ball some 25 yards out and after teeing himself up, he unleashes a powerful shot through a crowded penalty area and high past Fraser Forster into the top-right corner to put the Light Blues ahead.

4

7 August 2015

Lee Wallace gets Rangers' 2015/16 Scottish Championship campaign off and running as he opens the scoring against St Mirren at a sunny Ibrox. In what is new manager Mark Warburton's first home league game in charge, a corner from the right drops kindly for Wallace who thumps the ball into the roof of the net from seven yards out despite Saints claiming there had been a foul on Jack Beard.

5

20 October 1971

Colin Stein gets Rangers off to a terrific start as he opens the scoring against Sporting Lisbon. The first leg of the European Cup Winners' Cup second round tie at Ibrox drew a crowd of 50,000 as the Light Blues chased a first European success and Stein's effort makes it 1-0.

20 March 2005

On the tenth anniversary of Davie Cooper's death, Rangers start the Scottish League Cup Final in style with a smartly worked opening goal against Motherwell. Thomas Buffel spots right-back Maurice Ross's dart in from the flank and feeds a pass into his path. As two defenders and the goalkeeper come towards Ross, he calmly sends an angled lob over all of them and into the left-hand corner of the net to put the Light Blues 1-0 up.

15 May 2011

Rangers quickly double the lead away to Kilmarnock in a game the Light Blues must win to secure the Scottish Premier League title. Having gone ahead inside the first minute, there is more joy for the thousands of travelling fans as Gregg Wylde races down the left flank before finding Kai Naismith on the edge of the Killie box. Naismith turns on a sixpence before finishing with a low drive inside the right-hand post from 18 yards out to make it 2-0 at Rugby Park.

15 May 2021

Aberdeen keeper Joe Lewis attempts to cut out a James Tavernier cross from the right but as it takes a deflection the Dons skipper gets it all wrong and instead palms the ball into his own net to put the unbeaten champions on the way at Ibrox.

6

31 March 1992

Rangers fans fear the worst when David Robertson is shown a red card just six minutes into the Scottish Cup semi-final Old Firm clash with Celtic at Hampden Park. The Hoops' keeper throws the ball out for a quick counter-attack and as Joe Miller pushes it past Robertson near the halfway line, the left-back wipes out Miller with a forceful body check. After considering the punishment, referee Andrew Waddell sends Robertson for an early bath, though there is little doubt the Celtic player makes the most of the foul.

29 November 1998

Stéphane Guivarc'h gives Rangers an early lead against St Johnstone in the Scottish League Cup Final. The game, played at Celtic Park, explodes into life when a long ball is played down the right and into the path of Andrei Kanchelskis and the Ukrainian winger bursts into the box before playing a subtle pass back from the byline to Guivarc'h, who had cleverly held his run to create space and he lashes his shot past the keeper from five yards out to make it 1-0 – though the Saints equalise almost immediately.

6 October 2002

In what will be a six-goal thriller, Mikel Arteta puts Rangers 1-0 up at Celtic Park. Joos Valgaeren clears Fernando Ricksen's deflected shot to just outside the box where Spaniard Arteta scuffs a 25-yard daisy cutter that looks set to be easily scooped up by Hoops keeper Rab Douglas – but he somehow allows it to squirm under his body and into the net to put the Light Blues ahead.

23 January 2021

Ryan Kent gets the Gers off to a great start as he makes it 1-0 against Ross County at Ibrox. Having dropped points against Motherwell the week before, the Light Blues are keen to get back to winning ways and after James Tavernier picks out Alfredo Morelos, who heads the ball back across goal, Kent cleverly loops a header into the top corner and claims his seventh of the campaign.

7

15 May 1963

There is a sense of déjà vu when Rangers take the lead in the Scottish Cup Final replay. Celtic clearly hadn't learned their lesson from just 12 days before as the Gers score an almost carbon copy opening goal as Willie Henderson's low cross from the right sees Ralph Brand dart towards the near post where he turns the ball home to make it 1-0. The similarity is uncanny.

8 April 2000

Sebastián Rozental volleys Rangers into an early lead against First Division Ayr United in the Scottish Cup semi-final at Hampden Park. Ayr had seen off Dundee, Motherwell and Partick Thistle on their way to the semi-final but the Gers are a different animal completely and when Rod Wallace chases a long ball into the box on the left, his clever lobbed cross is turned in by Rozental to make it 1-0.

2 February 2005

Rangers get off to a fantastic start against Dundee United in the Scottish League Cup semi-final. The Light Blues have been lively from the kick-off and when Dado Pršo receives the ball on the right flank just inside his own half, he plays a superb first-time pass into the path of Nacho Novo, who skips past the onrushing keeper on the edge of the box before striking a low shot with the outside of his boot that the chasing defenders cannot keep out.

15 May 2011

Rangers' incredible start to the game away to Kilmarnock shifts up another gear. With victory needed on the final day at Rugby Park to secure the Scottish Premier League title, any pre-match nerves among the players or thousands of travelling fans are put to bed inside seven minutes as Kyle Lafferty scores his second to put the Light Blues 3-0 up. Nikica Jelavić is the provider, playing a low cross to Lafferty on the left edge of the box and the Northern Irishman coolly slots the ball under the keeper to seemingly wrap up the championship in no time at all.

26 November 2020

Scott Arfield opens the scoring against Benfica after two of his team-mates had gone desperately close in the same attack. Borna Barišić sends in yet another superb cross from the left and Alfredo Morelos's point-blank header is wonderfully saved by Benfica keeper Helton Leite – but the ball is pushed up and James Tavernier is on hand to thump a header against the woodwork before Arfield collects the loose ball and makes no mistake to put the Gers 1-0 up in the Europa League group stage clash at Ibrox.

8

29 April 1953

A superb move sees Rangers take the lead in the 1953 Scottish Cup Final against Aberdeen. At a sunny and packed Hampden Park – there are close to 130,000 people in attendance – the Gers score when Johnny Hubbard plays the ball out to his left and John Prentice send a low, left-footed shot into the bottom-right corner of the box to make it 1-0.

4 October 2009

Kenny Miller gets Rangers off to a terrific start in the first Old Firm clash of the 2009/10 Scottish Premier League campaign. Celtic arrived at Ibrox unbeaten and four points clear of their Glasgow rivals but all that will change in this game with Miller racing on to Kris Boyd's through ball and beating Artur Boruc with a composed low drive to put the Light Blues a goal to the good.

9

20 March 2005

January transfer signing Sotirios Kyrgiakos doubles Rangers' lead in the Scottish League Cup Final. The Greek defender comes up for a corner which is taken short to Barry Ferguson on the right of the Motherwell penalty area. Ferguson sends a teasing cross into the six-yard box and as keeper Gordon Marshall goes to collect it, midfielder Phil O'Donnell heads it over him and Kyrgiakos nods into the empty net from a couple of yards out to make it 2-0 with less than ten minutes on the clock.

17 October 2020

Rangers take a vital and early lead against defending Scottish Premiership champions Celtic. Despite the lack of supporters at the behind-closed-doors clash at Celtic Park, Steven Gerrard's league leaders are clearly fired up and the opening goal comes from – inevitably – a superb James Tavernier assist as he floats a free kick into the Hoops box and as Shane Duffy plays Connor Goldson onside, the Light Blues defender glances a superb header past Vasilis Barkas to make it 1-0.

25 October 2020

Joe Aribo puts Rangers ahead against Livingston as the unbeaten Scottish Premiership leaders look to get another three points wrapped up in double quick time. Ianis Hagi steals possession and plays in Jermain Defoe, but he is denied by keeper Max Stryjek. Hagi is again on hand to collect the loose ball and the Romanian spots Aribo unmarked at the far post, whips in a low cross and Aribo taps into the empty net.

25 February 2021

A dreadful pass back by a Royal Antwerp defender allows Ryan Kent to nip in and steal the ball, rounding the keeper in the process before pulling it back to the waiting Alfredo Morelos. The Colombian tucks home into the empty net to put the Light Blues 1-0 up in the Europa League round of 32 second leg at Ibrox and 5-3 up on aggregate.

10

20 October 1971

Colin Stein doubles Rangers' lead against Sporting Lisbon at Ibrox. Stein, who had opened the scoring on five minutes, sends Ibrox wild with a well-taken second as the Light Blues look to build a healthy first-leg lead in the European Cup Winners' Cup second round.

12 May 1981

Davie Cooper gives Rangers the lead in the 1981 Scottish Cup Final replay at Hampden Park. After the first game ended 0-0 four days earlier, the replay takes just ten minutes to spark into life as the ball pings around the edge of the Dundee United box before falling to Derek Johnstone who deftly lays it off to Cooper. Cooper controls the pass on his thigh as he runs into the box and then delicately lifts a shot over United keeper Hamish McAlpine and the ball trickles over the line to make it 1-0.

27 August 1988

Rangers get back on level terms with Celtic as Ally McCoist makes it 1-1 at Ibrox. In an early season league clash between the Glasgow rivals, the visitors had taken an early lead but following an almighty goalmouth scramble, the ball eventually falls to McCoist who doesn't strike his shot cleanly but it has just enough power to sneak inside the right post.

7 December 2002

Rangers recover from falling behind after just 19 seconds against Celtic in an explosive start to the Scottish Premier

League clash at Ibrox. Chris Sutton had put the Hoops ahead in the first attack of the game, but Gers strike back quickly. After winning a corner on the left, Fernando Ricksen sends a cross into the box and Craig Moore rises to power a header home and make it 1-1 with just ten minutes gone.

18 April 2021

The 36-year-old Steven Davis belies his age to score an acrobatic overhead kick and put Rangers 1-0 up against Celtic in the Scottish Cup fourth round. Joe Aribo picks up the ball after referee Bobby Madden plays advantage after Ryan Kent is fouled by Stephen Welsh 30 yards out. Aribo weaves inside and his shot loops up off Kristoffer Ajer and Davis, back to goal, sends a bicycle kick past Celtic keeper Scott Bain to score his second goal of the season.

11

24 November 1996

A delightful mazy run in from the right flank by Brian Laudrup sees the Dane find Ally McCoist on the edge of the Hearts box. McCoist has time to control the pass before hitting a measured low shot into the bottom-right corner to make it 1-0 against Hearts in the Scottish League Cup Final at Celtic Park. A polished goal from a striker at the peak of his powers.

24 March 2012

Strife-torn Rangers host Celtic with a determination not to let the Hoops win the Scottish Premier League title at Ibrox for the first time in 45 years, and strike first in the latest Old Firm battle. And what a goal it is as Sone Aluko dribbles his way towards the Celtic box before cutting inside of a challenge near the edge of the box and drilling a low shot into the bottom-left corner to put the Light Blues 1-0 up.

12

8 March 1972

Willie Johnston scores a priceless early goal in the European Cup Winners' Cup quarter-final, first leg against Torino. The Italians, playing on home soil, are stunned by Rangers' tenacity and the goal is the first conceded by Torino, who had kept clean sheets in both legs in each of the previous two rounds. The game will end 1-1 to leave the tie finely poised ahead of the second leg.

2 May 1999

On a day Rangers can make history by winning the Scottish Premier League title at Celtic Park for the first time, they grab the all-important first goal of what will be an explosive game. The early strike comes as Jorg Albertz releases Giovanni van Bronckhorst, who then pushes the ball on to Rod Wallace. Wallace races clear on the left and into the box and his knee-high cross is volleyed home by Neil McCann from six yards to give the Light Blues a crucial early advantage.

7 December 2013

Rangers look to record a 20th competitive victory and maintain a 100 per cent start to life in Scottish League One against Ayr United at Ibrox. It isn't long before the runaway leaders strike. After winning a free kick outside the box, Ian Black floats a cross in where Jon Daly rises to glance the ball past the keeper and make it 1-0.

27 September 2020

The Light Blues go ahead away to Motherwell after the ref awards a penalty for handball – Rangers' first spot-kick in 11 months. Calvin Bassey's cross from the left is flicked on by Scott Arfield and against the arm of Bevis Mugabi stood behind him. The ref immediately points to the spot, although it looks a tad harsh, and James Tavernier nets his fifth goal in six games to make it 1-0.

13

29 September 2012

Rangers' early entry into the Scottish Cup throws up a fascinating trip to Forres Mechanics in the second round. It is yet another outpost of Scottish football for the Glasgow giants, still getting to grips with life in the bottom division. The Highland champions prove tough opponents, too, with Kai Naismith's cool finish on 13 minutes following a terrific run and cross from Fraser Aird ultimately all that will separate two teams who couldn't be farther apart in terms of size, resource, and history – but are well matched in effort on the day. The game is played in front of a capacity crowd of 2,751 at Mosset Park.

12 September 2020

Terrific play by Ryan Kent gives Scottish Premiership leaders Rangers a 1-0 lead on what will be a long afternoon for Dundee United at Ibrox. Ianis Hagi receives the ball from Kent just outside the left-hand side of the box. The Romanian nutmegs a defender to return the ball to Kent who has carried on his run into the penalty area and after shaping to shoot with his right, Kent cuts back on to his left before drilling a low shot through the keeper's legs.

23 January 2021

What has become a goal drought for the prolific James Tavernier continues with his second successive penalty miss. The Light Blues are awarded a spot-kick against Ross County when Alfredo Morelos is fouled in the box but the skipper sees his effort saved by Ross Laidlaw and the score stays 1-0.

14

23 October 1988

Almost a year to the day from a dramatic Scottish League Cup Final between Rangers and Aberdeen, the two teams again lock horns at the same stage in a bid to win the trophy. The Gers had made the League Cup their own during the 1980s with five triumphs – including a 3-3 against the Dons and penalty shoot-out win 12 months before – and this will prove another absorbing encounter. After a dreadful error by Aberdeen keeper Theo Snelders results in a penalty, Ally McCoist steps up to put the Light Blues ahead from the spot.

25 October 1992

Stuart McCall takes advantage of some kamikaze Aberdeen defending to put Rangers ahead in the Scottish League Cup Final at Hampden Park. Gary Smith hits a loose ball back towards his own keeper at pace and Theo Snelders, unable to pick it up, instead chests the ball down and McCall runs in to jab a low shot home from close range to make it 1-0. It was shortly after the new rule had come in about keepers not picking up back passes so the Dutch keeper could be forgiven for the confusion.

6 March 2021

Rangers take the lead with another super Ryan Kent goal against St Mirren at Ibrox. Knowing that victory will put the Light Blues within a point of the Scottish Premiership title, Kent picks up the ball outside the Buddies' box, turns one way and then twists the other before sending a howitzer of a shot that arrows into the right of the net to make it 1-0.

15

29 August 2020

Ianis Hagi scores the opener for Scottish Premiership leaders Rangers away to Hamilton Academical. The unbeaten Light Blues – yet to concede a league goal in six games – strike when Borna Barišić finds Steven Davis on the left and his excellent cross is thumped against the bar by Kemar Roofe, but before the Accies defence can clear, Hagi pounces to prod home from close range and make it 1-0.

22 November 2020

Ryan Kent's sixth goal of the 2020/21 campaign is also arguably his best. The former Liverpool winger collects the ball on the left before nutmegging his marker and moves towards goal before unleashing a 25-yard shot that hits the right-hand post and flies into the back of the net to put the Light Blues 1-0 up against Aberdeen at Ibrox.

16

25 May 2003

On the final day of the 2002/03 Scottish Premier League title race, Rangers had been stunned by Dunfermline Athletic who had equalised Michael Mols's early goal. In a game where the Gers need to stack up the goals to win the title and better Celtic's goal difference, sanity is restored on 16 minutes when terrific work by Fernando Ricksen – chasing a ball that was going out for a goal kick and crossing to Claudio Caniggia at the same time – presents the Argentine with a simple opportunity from eight yards that he merely passes into the net to make it 2-1.

4 October 2009

Kenny Miller gets his second goal against Celtic with only 16 minutes of the Scottish Premier League Old Firm clash played. The Light Blues had come into the game on the back of three successive 0-0 draws in the league, but former Hoops striker Miller looks determined to single-handedly put that right as he latches on to Allan McGregor's long punt forward, outmuscles Glenn Loovens and manages to get away from two more chasing defenders before placing a low shot past Artur Boruc, who gets a hand to his effort but can't stop it going into the back of the net to make it 2-0 at an ecstatic Ibrox.

17 April 2016

Promotion-bound Rangers grab an early lead in the Scottish Cup semi-final at Hampden Park in a frantic Old Firm battle.

The breakthrough comes when James Tavernier's poor corner sees the ball go to Andy Halliday whose cross is misjudged by Scott Brown and Kenny Miller makes no mistake with the gift that is presented to him with a smart close-range finish.

25 October 2020

A wonderful moment for English striker Jermain Defoe as he scores his 300th career goal to give Rangers a 2-0 lead over Livingston at Ibrox – and what a sublime finish it is. Just as they did for the first goal, Livingston are again guilty of being sloppy in possession and Gers win the ball around the halfway line before working it across to skipper James Tavernier on the right. He looks up and plays a superb 40-yard pass into the path of Defoe, who caresses the ball as it lands into the most deft volley finish imaginable to give the keeper no chance. Brilliant from the veteran striker and brilliant from the captain.

8 November 2020

Jermain Defoe capitalises on a defensive mix-up between two Hamilton Academical defenders to spin and put a ball into the path of Ryan Kent down the left channel. Kent uses his pace to burst into the box before squaring it to Scott Arfield, who places a low shot past the keeper from ten yards out – all too easy for the Scottish Premiership leaders.

6 March 2021

Alfredo Morelos scores Rangers' second goal in the space of three minutes to edge them ever closer to a first Scottish Premiership title in ten years. Glen Kamara finds the Colombian in the box and his crisp shot across the keeper hits the far post and goes in for his 15th of the campaign to make it 2-0 at Ibrox.

17

30 November 1960

When Ralph Brand puts Rangers 2-0 up against Borussia Mönchengladbach in the second leg of the European Cup Winners' Cup second leg at Ibrox, it seems a matter of by how many rather than just if the Light Blues will win the game. Brand's goal puts the Gers 5-0 up on aggregate and on course for a big win against the Germans.

25 April 2010

With Celtic losing to Dundee United earlier in the day, Rangers know victory away to Hibernian will secure the Scottish Premier League title at Easter Road. In what will be a hard-fought 90 minutes, the only goal of the game comes when Kenny Miller chips the ball into the path of Kyle Lafferty to run on to and the Northern Ireland international holds off the challenges of Darren McCormack and Chris Hogg before thumping a left-footed drive into the corner of the net to make it 1-0. The victory means Celtic – 11 points adrift in second – cannot catch the Gers with just three games remaining.

10 April 2016

Championship winners Rangers take a fortuitous lead against Peterhead in the Scottish Challenge Cup – a trophy the Light Blues had never won and one that excluded top tier sides. In front of a crowd of more than 48,000 at Hampden Park, Kenny Miller sends in a low cross that Peterhead's Ally Gilchrist turns past his own keeper to put Rangers 1-0 up against the Aberdeenshire part-timers.

4 October 2020

A James Tavernier penalty gives Rangers a 1-0 lead over Ross County at Ibrox. The skipper bags his eighth in eight games after Alfredo Morelos is bundled over in the box by Coll Donaldson as he looks to get on the end of a Tavernier cross. Referee Greg Aitken points to the spot and Tavernier sends the keeper the wrong way.

18

25 November 1999

Rangers get a huge slice of good fortune against Borussia Dortmund in the first leg of the UEFA Cup fourth round. Dortmund skipper Jürgen Kohler tries to steer a cross from Gabriel Amato back to his keeper but skews the ball into his own net to give Gers a 1-0 lead at Ibrox.

2 February 2005

A superb header from Dado Pršo makes it 2-0 to Rangers in the Scottish League Cup semi-final clash with Dundee United. Marvin Andrews punts a long free kick into the Tangerines' box and Pršo, still with plenty to do, out-jumps his marker and connects with a diagonal header from 15 yards which somehow evades the keeper and goes in off the far post.

8 November 2020

Hamilton must fear they are in for a long afternoon at Ibrox as they ship a second goal in three minutes. Kemar Roofe does the damage as he heads powerfully past the Accies' keeper after a fine cross from the right by James Tavernier to make it 2-0.

19

22 October 2020

Skipper James Tavernier gets Rangers' Europa League group stage campaign off to a solid start as he opens the scoring from the penalty spot. Playing away to Standard Liège on a wet Belgian evening, the referee points to the spot after Liège's Nicolas Gavory handles a Connor Goldson header. Tavernier tucks away the resulting penalty by placing the ball in the bottom-left corner to make it 1-0.

1 November 2020

Prolific right-back James Tavernier's superb campaign continues to get better and better as the Light Blues' skipper scores what will be the only goal of the game away to Kilmarnock to ensure Steven Gerrard's side remain unbeaten in the league. Borna Barišić's free kick from inside Killie's half is met by Connor Goldson but Ross Millen's raised hand strikes the ball and the referee points to the spot. Tavernier dispatches the penalty with his usual assuredness.

8 November 2020

A third goal in the space of four minutes leaves Hamilton Academical looking at a hefty Ibrox defeat. Joe Aribo is played in on the right of the Accies' box and as he cuts inside, his weak shot takes a deflection and trundles into the bottom-left corner as the visitors threaten to capitulate. It is the Gers' third 19th-minute goal of the 2020/21 season.

20

29 August 2020

James Tavernier puts the Gers firmly in the box seat away to Hamilton Academical in the Scottish Premiership. The hosts are still reeling from Ianis Hagi's opener five minutes previously as the skipper doubles the Light Blues' lead. Ryan Kent leaves Accies' Hakeem Odoffin behind with a fine turn on the left before sending a cross into the box that keeper Ryan Fulton can't hold and Tavernier is on hand to put the loose ball in the back of the net and in doing so, secure three points – even though there are still 70 minutes to play.

11 April 2021

Champions Rangers go 1-0 up against Hibs at Ibrox as Steven Gerrard's men focus on preserving an unbeaten Scottish Premiership record for 2020/21. Kemar Roofe's header from Borna Barišić's cross brings a fine save from Ofir Marciano. The Gers keep the pressure up and Alfredo Morelos sees his follow-up shot saved before the ball drops to Joe Aribo, who sends an angled volley into the left-hand corner to make it 1-0.

21

19 April 1972

Rangers double their lead against Bayern Munich in the European Cup Winners' Cup semi-final, second leg at Ibrox. Having gone ahead inside a minute through Sandy Jardine's spectacular long-range shot, Derek Parlane scores a beauty too as a corner comes in from the left from Willie Johnstone and he thumps a ferocious left-footed volley past West Germany keeper Sepp Maier into the roof of the net from ten yards to make it 2-0 and 3-1 on aggregate. It proves to be enough to book Rangers a place in the final against Russian giants Dynamo Moscow and isn't a bad way for the 18-year-old to mark his European debut for the Gers.

12 May 1981

Bobby Russell emphatically blasts home to put Rangers 2-0 up in the Scottish Cup Final replay at Hampden Park. The goal comes as Davie Cooper floats a free kick into the Dundee United six-yard box from the left which finds Russell stealing in to volley a powerful, angled shot into the top-left corner of the net to give the keeper no chance and double the Light Blues' lead.

4 May 2002

Having just fallen behind to Celtic in the 2002 Scottish Cup Final, Rangers level almost immediately at Hampden Park. A long ball is played towards Peter Løvenkrands who is closely marked by two Celtic defenders on the right of the box. Both then go for the same header and Løvenkrands profits, picking up the loose ball and hitting a low, left-footed shot just inside the right-hand post to make it 1-1.

1 August 2020

Ryan Kent scores Rangers' opening goal of what will be a fantastic 2020/21 campaign with a strike that will also be enough to beat Aberdeen 1-0 at Pittodrie. As the ball is played to Alfredo Morelos on the halfway line, the Colombian slides an inch-perfect ball into the path of Kent – splitting the Dons' wide open defence apart in the process – and Kent is cool as a cucumber as he places a low shot to the keeper's right and into the bottom corner.

12 August 2020

Borna Barišić shows his set-piece quality yet again with a superb free kick against St Johnstone. The Croatian left-back, a bargain signing in 2018, breaks the deadlock in the Scottish Premiership clash at Ibrox with a beautiful curling effort from 22 yards that sails over the wall and into the top-right corner to make it 1-0 at Ibrox.

22

25 October 1987

Davie Cooper scores to make it 1-1 against Aberdeen in the Scottish League Cup Final at Hampden Park. The Dons had gone ahead after just nine minutes from a Jim Bett penalty, but when a free kick is awarded on the edge of the Aberdeen box, Cooper lashes a ferocious left-footed shot through the wall and into the top-left corner – another wonderful goal from the Rangers legend.

23

24 May 1972

Colin Stein opens the scoring in the European Cup Winners' Cup Final at Barcelona's Camp Nou with a superb strike. Chasing a long pass towards the Dynamo Moscow box from Dave Smith, Stein – who already had four goals in the competition – gets the ball under control inside the box before unleashing a thunderous shot into the roof of the net to make it 1-0 and spark a pitch invasion of delirious Rangers fans.

29 May 1993

Neil Murray puts Rangers ahead in the Scottish Cup Final after a disastrous few seconds for Aberdeen defender Brian Irvine. As a cross comes into the Dons' box from the left, Irvine makes a hash of his attempted clearance and the ball rolls to Murray. Desperate to make up for his mistake, Irvine then lunges at Murray's shot and deflects it past Theo Snelders to make it 1-0. Snelders must have felt a distinct sense of déjà vu as he had been beaten by one of his own defenders, Gary Smith, in the Scottish League Cup Final against Rangers earlier in the campaign.

16 March 2003

Rangers break the deadlock against Celtic in the Scottish League Cup Final. Ronald de Boer threads a pass into the run of Peter Løvenkrands Rab Douglas parries his angled shot across goal and Claudio Caniggia is first to the loose ball, placing it wide of Bobo Baldé's despairing attempt to clear and making it 1-0.

19 September 2010

Sheyi Ojo scores a thunderbolt of a goal to give the Gers a 1-0 lead over Feyenoord at Ibrox. On an emotional evening following the death of former skipper Fernando Ricksen the previous day, James Tavernier had missed from the penalty spot early on in the Europa League group stage clash with the Dutch giants. But Ojo makes amends for his captain when he collects the ball on the left of the box and seems intent on one thing – shooting – which he does from 20 yards with a left-footed fizzer that gives the keeper no chance. It will be the only goal of the game.

27 September 2011

Steven Naismith continues his impressive early season form with a stunning goal to put defending champions Rangers 1-0 up against Celtic. In a typically feisty Old Firm Scottish Premier League clash, the Light Blues strike first as a low cross into the Celtic box is only half-cleared to Naismith on the right-hand side and he controls the ball, then bends a superb rising shot into the top-left corner with the outside of his right boot to send Ibrox crazy.

8 August 2020

Rangers go 1-0 up against St Mirren via an own goal from the visitors. In the opening Ibrox game of the 2020/21 campaign, Steven Gerrard's men continue a 100 per cent start with the first of three against Saints. Glen Kamara spots Alfredo Morelos in space inside the box and the Colombian's shot across goal is turned past his own keeper by Conor McCarthy.

24

5 April 1947

Torry Gillick puts Rangers ahead in the first Scottish League Cup Final, against Aberdeen. The Dons, also fighting for the league title, Scottish Cup and League Cup, fall behind when the 31-year-old Gillick – enjoying a second spell with the Light Blues – scores the opener at Hampden Park, much to the delight of the majority of the 82,700 crowd.

4 November 2000

Rangers double the lead against St Mirren in a one-sided Scottish Premier League clash at Ibrox. Kenny Miller – who scored the opener inside two minutes – is on the mark again as Ronald de Boer plays a pass inside the St Mirren full-back for Arthur Numan to scamper down the left flank and his cross is bundled home at the far post by Miller to make it 2-0.

20 March 2011

In the 14th Scottish League Cup Final between Rangers and Celtic, it is the Light Blues – chasing a ninth Old Firm success at this stage – who open the scoring at Hampden Park. In what will be Walter Smith's last showpiece final as boss, the Gers have the added incentive of stopping Celtic from winning a possible treble. Steven Davis is as determined as anyone as he drives towards the Hoops' box and despite a posse of defenders ahead of him, he fires a low, left-footed shot that has just enough power to sneak past Fraser Forster via the right-hand post and into the net to make it 1-0.

12 March 2014

Lee McCulloch gets his second goal of the game against Airdrie – and his second penalty inside 24 minutes as the Gers head towards the Scottish League One title in a canter. David Templeton is brought down in the box by Gregor Buchanan and the referee once more points to the spot. McCulloch again makes no mistake and it is 2-0.

5 November 2020

In an incident-packed game away to Benfica in the Europa League group stage, Rangers level the scores. The hosts had gone ahead inside the first minute, then had Nicolás Otamendi dismissed on 19 before the Light Blues strike. In keeping with the colourful nature of what had gone before, an own goal gives Gers parity. Steven Davis sends James Tavernier clear down the right flank and his square pass is blasted past his own keeper by Diogo Gonçalves to make it 1-1.

23 December 2020

Rangers' march towards the title continues as Kemar Roofe prods home the opener away to St Johnstone. Glen Kamara moves into the Saints' half with purpose before picking out Ianis Hagi on the edge of the box. Hagi's low drive is palmed out by the keeper but Roofe is in like a flash to net the loose ball for his seventh in six games.

25

4 November 2000

Kenny Miller completes a 25-minute hat-trick against St Mirren to make it 3-0 at Ibrox. In his third game for the club, he shows why he will become a big crowd favourite when he leaps to head Jorg Albertz's cross past keeper Derek Scrimgour following a swift counter-attack to make it 3-0.

25 October 2015

Rangers' perfect start to life in the Scottish Championship continues – just – with a hard-fought 1-0 win away to St Mirren. Mark Warburton's side record an 11th successive win as Jason Holt squeezes an angled shot home to put the Gers eight points clear of second-placed Hibs.

13 May 2018

Chasing a runners-up spot in the Scottish Premiership, Rangers trail Hibs 3-0 with just 22 minutes played at Easter Road. But James Tavernier's goal on 25 gives the Light Blues hope – though nobody could have guessed the flood of goals this game would produce on the final day of the campaign. Jason Holt's low cross from the right of the box is swept home by Tavernier to make it 3-1 in Hibs' favour but it will spark an incredible comeback by the visitors.

5 November 2020

Rangers grab a second goal inside a minute to lead 2-1 away to Benfica. Alfredo Morelos races down the right before hitting a crossfield ball to Glen Kamara who controls the pass, cuts in from the left and drills a fierce low drive inside Benfica keeper Odysseas Vlachodimos's near post to make it 2-1 in a wide open and entertaining Europa League group stage clash in Portugal.

26

3 November 1971

Rangers hit back within two minutes of going behind away to Sporting Lisbon. The Portuguese giants – who had at one stage trailed 3-0 on aggregate in the tie – had gone 1-0 up in front of a fanatical crowd of 60,000 at the Estádio José Alvalade to make it 3-3 overall and lead on away goals, but Colin Stein, who bagged two in the first leg at Ibrox, equalises by ramming home a low drive to put the Light Blues back in command.

7 December 2013

The Gers double their lead against Ayr United with a smart strike from Fraser Aird. Chasing a 20th consecutive win, Ally McCoist's side are focused on closing in on the club record of 22 victories in succession and Aird's goal puts the Light Blues well on the way towards that. Collecting a ball out of defence from Bilel Mohsni, Aird looks set to play it out wide, but instead keeps possession and then hits a crisp shot past the keeper from 20 yards to make it 2-0.

7 August 2015

Lee Wallace's start to the 2015/16 Scottish Championship just gets better and better as he bags his second opening-day goal to give the Gers a 2-0 lead against St Mirren. James Holt threads a pass through to Wallace on the left of the Saints' box and the Light Blues' skipper hits an angled shot past the keeper to the delight of the 49,216 Ibrox crowd.

13 December 2020

James Tavernier scores his 17th of the season with a stunning free kick away to Dundee United. The irrepressible Rangers skipper, in the form of his life, equals his own career-best seasonal tally as the Gers are awarded a free kick some 30 yards from goal. Borna Barišić and Tavernier stand over the ball but it is the captain who takes it, floating a delightful shot into the top-left corner to make it 1-0 at Tannadice.

2 May 2021

Kemar Roofe puts Rangers 1-0 up in the Scottish Premiership Old Firm clash with Celtic at Ibrox. With the title already wrapped up, the Light Blues are keen to further rub salt in the wounds of the Hoops and the opening goal comes after good advantage is played by the referee, who allows an attack to continue as the ball is worked to the left for Aribo. His precise pass back to the edge of the box finds Ryan Kent who hits a ball towards goal where Roofe expertly guides a chested effort into the left of the net from eight yards with the keeper left flat-footed. The referee then shows Callum McGregor a second yellow to reduce the visitors to ten men with more than two-thirds of the game remaining.

27

24 November 1996

Rangers double their lead against Hearts in the Scottish League Cup Final at Celtic Park. The goal comes from a deep corner from the left that finds the head of Gordan Petrić, who nods it across the six-yard box where Craig Moore then heads it towards Ally McCoist who heads past the keeper from a yard or so out to make it 2-0.

8 April 2000

Andrei Kanchelskis doubles Rangers' lead in the Scottish Cup semi-final against Ayr United. The First Division outfit have given an excellent account of themselves at Hampden Park, but Arthur Numan's cross is nodded on to Kanchelskis – full of confidence and with some outrageous showboating – who brings the ball down, shimmies one way then comes back inside and rolls a low shot past the keeper to put the Light Blues 2-0 up.

13 February 2003

Rangers take the lead in the Scottish League Cup semi-final against Hearts. Neil McCann's cross from the left flank picks out the head of Fernando Ricksen and the Dutch defender's nod back across goal allows compatriot Ronald de Boer to thump a header past Hearts keeper Tepi Moilanen to make it 1-0. It will prove to be the only goal of the game and sends Gers into a final against Celtic.

11 August 2012

An historic day and an historic moment as 17-year-old Barrie McKay scores Rangers' first Scottish Third Division goal. Having been effectively booted out of Scottish football, Rangers had been voted back into the league under strict regulations having been found guilty of financial irregularities. The Light Blues had to start over in the bottom tier and open with a trip to Aberdeenshire to face Peterhead. McKay's strike comes when a ball into the box is only cleared to the edge where he collects and sweeps a low shot home to put Ally McCoist's side in front.

13 May 2018

Rangers score for a second time in three minutes as Hibs see a three-goal lead reduced to just one. Jamie Murphy's probing outside the box results in a fine through ball to Jordan Rossiter who takes a touch before tucking home a low shot to make it 3-2 and keep the Light Blues' hopes of finishing runners-up to Celtic – and more importantly pipping Aberdeen to a Champions League spot – very much alive.

30 December 2020

Rangers break the deadlock away to St Mirren with a goal out of nothing. Ianis Hagi is quick to pounce on a mistake by Jamie McGrath of St Mirren and slips the ball to Kemar Roofe inside the box. Roofe has one thing in his mind as he pushes the ball forward before striking an angled shot that takes a slight deflection as it loops up and over Saints keeper Jak Alnwick to make it 1-0 to Gers.

28

27 September 2020

A fantastic move from Rangers doubles the lead away to Motherwell, who can't cope with the slick passing and movement of the Scottish Premiership leaders. A series of quick passes ends with Scott Arfield playing a precise ball through to Jordan Jones, who drives in from the right flank, uses his pace to get behind the Well defence and then clips a left-footed shot in off the right post for his first goal for the club.

6 December 2020

A terrific move finally dissects a resolute Ross County defence to put the Light Blues 1-0 up in the Highlands. The hosts had gone closest to scoring earlier in the half but fall behind when Steven Davis plays a superb pass inside the Ross full-back for James Tavernier, who fizzes a low cross into the six-yard box for Kemar Roofe to expertly slide home his eighth of the season.

23 January 2021

Filip Helander's powerful header doubles the Gers' lead against Ross County at Ibrox. Borna Barišić's corner finds the head of the Swede who gives the keeper no chance as he makes it 2-0. Such is the non-existent marking by the visitors that Helander probably could have closed his eyes and still scored, given the space and time he had.

29

12 May 1981

The brilliant Davie Cooper – who had already scored one and created one – claims another superb assist as Rangers go 3-1 up in the Scottish Cup Final replay against Dundee United at Hampden Park. Picking up a poor clearance by the United defence, Cooper, 30 yards out, drifts past one challenge then another as he comes in from the right flank and then spots the run of John McDonald on the left. Cooper threads a low pass into McDonald's path to put him clear on goal and he finishes with a low shot past the keeper to put the Gers firmly in command.

22 November 2020

Rangers go 2-0 up against Aberdeen at Ibrox with a goal that the Aberdeen defence probably wouldn't want to watch a replay of. Connor Goldson plays an excellent lofted ball into the feet of Kemar Roofe, who controls it as it lands and goes past one challenge – but looks set to lose possession only for a weak challenge to be brushed off – and then sends in a left-footed shot that the keeper makes a hash of as it goes into the net.

30

3 May 1967

Having somehow come away from Bulgaria with a 1-0 victory in the European Cup Winners' Cup semi-final, first leg, Rangers know there is more hard work to do at Ibrox if a second major European final is to be reached. Slavia Sofia, a technical and talented side, should have arrived in Glasgow with a healthy lead, such was their dominance in the first leg, but again they are foiled by a determined Rangers who will grab the only goal of the game on the half-hour when a cross is cleared to the edge of the Sofia box and Willie Henderson thumps a left-footed half-volley into the top-right corner from the edge of the box to send the sell-out Ibrox crowd wild and book a place in the final against Bayern Munich after a 2-0 aggregate win.

20 October 1971

Winger Willie Henderson scores a superb long-range effort as Rangers open up a 3-0 lead over Sporting Lisbon. The European Cup Winners' Cup second round first leg at an electric Ibrox looks done and dusted with the Portuguese struggling to cope with the Light Blues' constant pressure. Henderson will later claim the goal was one of the best of his career. However, Sporting will score twice before the end of the game to put the tie on a knife edge.

9 May 1992

After 11 years without winning the Scottish Cup, Rangers take the lead in the final against Airdrie at Hampden Park.

The Scottish Premier League champions – who finished with exactly double the points Airdrie had (72 to 36) – start as strong favourites but have to wait until the half-hour to edge ahead when left-back David Robertson collects a crossfield pass and as the Airdrie defender marking him slips, he has plenty of time and space to pick out the run of Mark Hateley and the England striker makes no mistake with a near-post finish to make it 1-0.

25 May 2003

Rangers go 3-1 up at Ibrox against Dunfermline Athletic. Needing a handsome win to ensure Celtic don't snatch the Scottish Premier League title on goal difference on the final day of the campaign, Lorenzo Amoruso shows the commitment needed of champions as he chases an over-hit cross and keeps the ball in play before turning and sending a lovely ball back into the middle where Shota Arveladze expertly glances a header across the keeper and into the right-hand corner to give the leaders breathing space.

20 December 2018

Rangers secure a 1-0 victory over Celtic to give Steven Gerrard his first Old Firm success and Hoops boss Brendan Rodgers his first defeat in 13 matches against the Light Blues. When the goal comes, it's fully deserved in what has been a one-sided affair. Celtic were ragged, and that sense of disorientation eventually proved costly. The lively Ryan Kent leaves Mikael Lustig on his backside with a fine run and turn down the left and his pass to Ryan Jack just inside the box sees the midfielder side-foot a shot through the legs of Scott Brown and off his heel to divert it away from Craig Gordon.

31

30 November 1960

Rangers go 3-0 up against Borussia Mönchengladbach just past the half-hour as Lambert Pfeiffer puts past his own goalkeeper on what will be a miserable night for the Germans. The goal effectively ends the game as a contest with the Gers now 6-0 up on aggregate and heading for the European Cup Winners' Cup semi-finals.

23 December 2020

Glen Kamara puts Rangers 2-0 up at St Johnstone with a superbly worked goal. Joe Aribo collects a Steven Davis header in midfield and then turns towards the Saints' defence. After a couple of strides he threads an inch-perfect ball into the path of Kamara who uses the weight of the pass to caress his shot past the onrushing keeper and into the net from just inside the box. Such an intricate goal made to look so simple.

15 May 2021

Kemar Roofe doubles Rangers' lead against Aberdeen on the final day of the 2020/21 campaign. The goal is a result of Ryan Kent's persistence and determination as he drives down the left touchline before forcing his way past two Aberdeen defenders and cutting back to Roofe, whose scuffed shot somehow finds its way past Joe Lewis to make it 2-0.

32

5 April 1947

The prolific Billy Williamson makes it two goals in eight minutes for Rangers who go 2-0 up against Aberdeen in the first Scottish League Cup Final. Torry Gillick had opened the scoring at Hampden Park and Williamson's strike gives Bill Struth's side a firm grip on the game.

4 November 2000

The Kenny Miller show continues as he bags his fourth in 30 minutes to put Gers 4-0 up against a woeful St Mirren. Barry Ferguson plays a clever pass towards Miller who hits a poor shot towards goal from eight yards out, but the keeper makes an ever poorer attempt to save it as it goes through his attempt and into the net on what will be a long and painful afternoon for the visitors from Paisley.

4 May 2012

Fraser Aird's header gives Scottish Third Division champions Rangers a 1-0 win over Berwick Rangers at Ibrox. With a crowd of 50,048 in attendance, the Gers' fans had embraced the lower-league adventure and though there had been some shock results along the way, a 24-point margin at the top meant the title had been wrapped up almost two months before the trophy would be lifted. Kyle Hutton's inswinging cross from the left is nodded in by Aird from just inside the six-yard box. It had been a season like no other, with the Light Blues playing sides such as Annan Athletic, Elgin City and East Stirling and no doubt many of the clubs left behind were sorry to see such a glamour fixture off their schedules so soon.

33

29 March 1961

Rangers and Wolverhampton Wanderers locked horns in a 'Battle of Britain' European Cup Winners' Cup semi-final first leg at Ibrox. The game had caught the imagination of the Gers' fans, with 80,000 packing into Ibrox to see if their team could become the first British side to reach a major European final. The breakthrough for the Light Blues comes on 33 minutes when the ball falls to Alex Scott who hits a sweet strike past the Wolves keeper to make it 1-0, much to the delight of the blue half of Glasgow.

24 May 2008

Kris Boyd spectacularly fires Rangers ahead in the 2008 Scottish Cup Final at Hampden Park against Queen of the South. When DaMarcus Beasley is fouled 25 yards from goal, it is Boyd who steps up to take the set piece and his powerful shot arrows like a missile into the top-right corner to give the Gers a 1-0 lead.

20 March 2005

Having scored against Aberdeen and Dundee United in the 2004/05 Scottish League Cup run, Rangers captain Fernando Ricksen saves his best effort for the final against Motherwell. From a free kick 25 yards out and on the left of the box, it looks ambitious as Ricksen runs up but he hits a perfect shot over the wall and inside the keeper's near post to put the Light Blues 3-1 up at Hampden Park.

26 December 2020

Ianis Hagi scores the only goal of the game as Rangers record a 12th straight Scottish Premiership victory to further strengthen their grip at the top. On a Boxing Day fixture at a still-empty Ibrox, Hagi brings festive cheer to the Light Blues' fans as he breaks down Hibs' stern resistance with a goal on 33 minutes. Glen Kamara and Joe Aribo create an opening after a smart one-two sees Kamara find Kemar Roofe on the left, and he holds off a challenge to cross into the middle where Hagi steals in to drill a low, left-footed shot into the bottom-right corner.

30 December 2020

A late Christmas present from former team-mate Joe Shaughnessy allows Alfredo Morelos in to put Rangers 2-0 up away to St Mirren and on the way to yet another victory. Shaughnessy receives the ball ten yards from his own box with Morelos lurking close by. The Colombian's presence is enough for the St Mirren defender to hurry his back pass, but he barely makes contact and Morelos runs on to collect the ball and place it past the keeper.

2 May 2021

Four minutes after Celtic had levelled the scores in the last Old Firm derby of the 2020/21 campaign, Rangers go 2-1 up at Ibrox. Borna Barišić sends in a cross from the left which is only half-cleared by the Celtic defence but the ball is played back into Alfredo Morelos, who cuts inside one defender before unleashing a ferocious angled shot that rockets into the roof of the net from ten yards out for a superb goal.

10 January 2021

Rangers take the lead at Pittodrie against ten-man Aberdeen. The Dons, having survived a rare penalty miss by James Tavernier, are made to pay by the skipper, who breezes past Jonny Hayes on the right before finding Ryan Kent in the box. He in turn lays it to Alfredo Morelos who turns his marker, spins around and drives a super low drive into the bottom-right corner to give the Scottish Premiership leaders a 1-0 lead in the Granite City. It is already Rangers' fourth goal on 33 minutes in the league during the 2020/21 season.

34

28 November 2015

Rangers finally take the lead against St Mirren in a one-sided Scottish Challenge Cup semi-final at Ibrox. The opener comes when Jason Holt's driving run is picked out by Andy Halliday's superb ball at the back post and he drills a low shot past the keeper to make it 1-0 on a wet and windy day in the South Side of Glasgow.

18 April 2021

Brilliant wing play by Joe Aribo sees Rangers go 2-0 up against Celtic in the Scottish Cup fourth round at Ibrox. The Old Firm clash, played behind closed doors due to COVID-19 restrictions, was a chance for the Light Blues to re-establish themselves as top dogs in Glasgow having already won the Scottish Premiership and prevented Celtic winning ten titles in a row. Aribo's trickery down the right, turning a defender inside out before waiting for the right moment to cross into the six-yard box where he spots Ryan Kent's run, leads to Jonjoe Kenny getting to the ball first and flashing it past his own keeper to make it 2-0 for the Gers and ensures the Hoops end the season without silverware for the first time in 11 years.

35

24 January 1973

Rangers re-take the lead in the second leg of the European Super Cup against Ajax. Having gone ahead early on but been pegged back by Arie Haan's leveller, they take advantage of a set piece to undo the Dutch giants. Tommy McLean curls a free kick into the box and Quintin Young dives in to head the Light Blues back in front – 2-1 on the night but still 4-3 down on aggregate. Ajax level almost from the kick-off and a Johan Cruyff winner on 79 gives them a 3-2 win on the night and a 6-3 aggregate victory.

5 May 1973

Rangers level against Celtic in the 1973 Scottish Cup Final. In what is the Light Blues' centenary year, Kenny Dalglish gives Celtic the lead in front of 122,714 fans at Hampden Park. But Alex MacDonald manages to get a cross in from the left and Derek Parlane – on his 20th birthday – is first to the ball, sending a smart low header past the keeper to make it 1-1.

6 May 1978

Rangers go 1-0 up against Aberdeen in the 1978 Scottish Cup Final. Bobby Russell is the creator, cutting in from the left and whipping a cross into the Dons' box where Alex MacDonald, bursting in, is able to get his head on to the ball which bobbles past keeper Bobby Clarke as he fumbles the effort.

27 August 1988

Ray Wilkins scores a stunning volley to put Rangers 2-1 up against Celtic in a league clash at Ibrox. A long throw into the Hoops' box is cleared to the edge of the area by the Celtic defence, but only as far as Wilkins who strikes a sweet volley from 20 yards that rockets past the keeper to send the Rangers fans wild. It is a wonderful goal by the cultured English midfielder and one of the best seen in an Old Firm game.

7 December 2002

Ronald de Boer puts Gers 2-1 up against Celtic at Ibrox. Neill McCann skips past Joos Valgaeren and Bobo Baldé before sending a delightful chip into the middle which Dutchman de Boer meets on the full to give keeper Rab Douglas no chance with a powerful volley into the roof of the net from six yards out.

16 March 2003

Rangers double their lead against Celtic in the Old Firm Scottish League Cup Final clash at Hampden Park. There's an element of déjà vu about the goal, with another threaded pass that splits the Hoops defence apart – this time played by Michael Mols – and again Peter Løvenkrands darts into the box, but this time he lifts a low shot over the dive of keeper Douglas to score and make it 2-0. It will prove decisive with the Light Blues winning 2-1.

21 February 2021

Rangers break the deadlock against Dundee United to go 1-0 up at Ibrox. Joe Aribo's trickery on the right of the box sees him torment a defender before firing a shot goalwards that

Ianis Hagi manages to get the merest of touches to, but it is enough to divert it away from the keeper and into the net.

36

19 April 1967

Quite how Rangers survived an onslaught from Slavia Sofia in the first leg of the European Cup Winners' Cup semi-final is something close to incredible. The hosts battered them in the opening half-hour with the woodwork, several incredible goalmouth scrambles, great goalkeeping from Norrie Martin and sheer luck keeping the Light Blues in the game. But this Rangers side has resilience by the bucketload and when a rare shot is spilled by the Sofia keeper, David Wilson is on hand to convert from close range to give the Gers a priceless away goal and a 1-0 victory to take back to Glasgow.

8 November 2020

Joe Aribo grabs his second of the game to put Rangers 4-0 up against a pretty woeful Hamilton Academical side. The Scottish Premiership leaders were already in cruise control against the visitors but, looking to bolster an already decent goal difference, the Light Blues are at their ruthless best. James Tavernier sends in one of his almost unplayable crosses from the right that manages to evade everyone, then Kemar Roofe retrieves the ball on the left of the six-yard box and then tees up Aribo who sees his shot take a deflection and float past the keeper into the net.

11 March 2021

Filip Helander grabs a vital away goal as Rangers take on Slavia Prague in the Europa League round of 16, first leg. The Czech side, who had beaten Leicester City in the previous round, had grabbed an early goal to lead 1-0, but the Light Blues level before the break from a set piece. Borna Barišić swings in a free kick and the ball deflects goalwards, but it seems to be going out of play until a deft touch from Ianis Hagi, who keeps it in play, allows Swedish defender Helander the simple task of tapping home to give Steven Gerrard's side a 1-1 draw to take back to Ibrox.

37

20 April 1935

Jimmy Smith gives league champions Rangers the lead in the Scottish Cup Final. Up against Hamilton Academical, who hadn't reached the final for 24 years, the Gers are thwarted by some excellent defending by the Lanarkshire club. But Smith finally breaks the deadlock much to the delight of the majority of the 87,740 Hampden Park crowd.

28 September 1971

Alex MacDonald scores what will be the only goal of the European Cup Winners' Cup first round, second leg in front of a 40,000 Ibrox crowd. The former St Johnstone midfielder's winner gives Rangers a 1-0 lead on the night and a 2-1 lead on aggregate – a lead the Light Blues will hold until full time to progress into the second round.

18 May 1996

Brian Laudrup puts Rangers 1-0 up in the Scottish Cup Final against Hearts. Chasing on to a lofted through pass, Laudrup wastes no time firing a crisp low shot across the Hearts keeper and into the bottom-left corner to make it 1-0 at Hampden Park.

29 November 1998

Rangers go back in front in the Scottish League Cup Final with a well-worked goal. St Johnstone had been feisty and difficult to break down but when Jorg Albertz is fed a pass 30 yards from goal, he plays a quick one-two with Stéphane

Guivarc'h before hitting a low shot into the bottom-right corner from 15 yards out. It proves to be the winner, too, with the Light Blues edging the game 2-1.

31 August 2008

Daniel Cousin scores a superb individual goal to put the Light Blues a goal up at Celtic Park. Pedro Mendes finds Cousin in space on the right flank and the striker then puts his head down, gliding past the Celtic full-back Mark Wilson as he runs into the box at an angle and as he closes in he fires a low shot that beats the keeper on his near post to put the Gers 1-0 up.

27 September 2020

James Tavernier's sixth goal in six games puts the Gers 3-0 up at Motherwell. Having not been awarded a penalty in the league for 11 months, the Light Blues get a second in 25 minutes. But if the first award for handball had been harsh, the second is less so as a corner comes in and Motherwell's Liam Grimshaw makes a bizarre clearance with his upper arm. Tavernier makes no mistake from the spot.

23 January 2021

Rangers wrap up the points against Ross County with a stunning third goal before half-time from Joe Aribo. The skilful Nigerian beats one defender on the right of the box before cutting inside another and curling a beauty into the left-hand corner of the net from a tight angle.

13 February 2021

For the fourth Scottish Premiership game in a row, unbeaten leaders Rangers can only score one goal – but it is enough to see off Kilmarnock 1-0 at a snowy and arctic Ibrox. And it is a goal worthy of winning any game as a goalmouth scramble sees the ball come to Ryan Jack 20 yards out, where he flips it up and then volleys it into the top-right corner.

38

18 March 1978

Ronnie Glavin's attempt to see the ball out for a goal kick allows Gordon Smith the chance to hook it back into the centre where Davie Cooper rushes in to fire a powerful shot past Celtic keeper Peter Latchford and put Rangers 1-0 up in the 1977/78 Scottish League Cup Final. Incredibly, the Hoops are playing in their 14th consecutive League Cup Final.

18 February 2021

Joe Aribo puts Rangers ahead before the break in the Europa League round of 32 first leg against Royal Antwerp. The Light Blues had been bright and positive throughout the opening period and the goal is just reward when it arrives. Kemar Roofe chases down a ball back towards the Antwerp keeper Alireza Beiranvand, which causes him to fumble the ball into the path of Alfredo Morelos. He attempts to block the Colombian on the edge of the box but Morelos manages to scramble the ball to Aribo, who hits a 20-yard shot past defenders and into the net to make it 1-0.

21 February 2021

Not the prettiest of goals Ryan Kent will ever score but it's enough to put Gers 2-0 up against Dundee United. As a cross from the left is headed clear, Kent is waiting on the edge of the box and his low volley hits the inside leg of a United defender and wrong-foots the keeper in the process.

21 March 2021

Alfredo Morelos grabs his first Old Firm goal to earn a 1-1 draw away to Celtic and preserve the Light Blues' unbeaten league record. Borna Barišić's corner is met by Leon Balogun who heads towards the far post where Morelos races in to bravely head home the equaliser.

39

23 April 1949

Billy Williamson is hacked down as he bursts through the Clyde defence and a penalty is awarded. Clyde had held out in the Scottish Cup Final up to that stage but George Young casually strokes the ball into the bottom-left corner to put Rangers 1-0 up at Hampden Park.

3 December 2020

Rangers level against Standard Liège. Connor Goldson thumps home a header from a Borna Barišić corner to give the keeper no chance in a game the Light Blues look to seal a place in the Europa League round of 32.

12 September 2020

Rangers' two deadly full-backs combine yet again to open up a 2-0 lead over Dundee United at Ibrox. Left-back Borna Barišić sends in a typically tempting cross that evades all except skipper James Tavernier, who slides the ball home at the far post on his 250th appearance for the Light Blues.

40

5 April 1947

Jimmy Duncanson puts Rangers 3-0 up and within sight of winning the Scottish League Cup at the very first attempt. The new trophy, eagerly backed by supporters with more than 82,000 at Hampden Park, looks certain to head back to Ibrox as Duncanson makes no mistake with a clinical finish to make it three goals in the space of 16 minutes for Bill Struth's side.

21 April 1962

Ralph Brand bundles the ball home to give Rangers a 1-0 lead in the Scottish Cup Final against St Mirren. Dave Wilson's low cross sees Brand and St Mirren's John Wilson battle for the ball and when Wilson falls, Brand has the simple task of tucking the ball past the keeper.

24 October 1970

Rangers claim a seventh Scottish League Cup success with a single-goal victory over Celtic at Hampden Park. Celtic start as favourites, but the Light Blues adapt to the sodden conditions better and score on 40 minutes when Willie Henderson slips as he sends over a fine inswinging cross from the right wing and as Hoops defenders McNeill and Craig hesitate, 16-year-old Derek Johnstone rises to send a bullet header down into the bottom-left corner past the diving Evan Williams to make it 1-0 in front of a mammoth 106,263 crowd.

24 May 1972

The impressive Dave Smith claims his second assist of the 1972 European Cup Winners' Cup Final as Rangers go 2-0 up against Dynamo Moscow. Smith advances into the Moscow half before cutting in slightly and curling a cross into the box where Willie Johnston leaps to guide a header into the bottom-left corner at Barcelona's Camp Nou.

25 October 1987

Wonderful combination play between Ian Durrant and Ally McCoist gives Rangers a 2-1 lead over Aberdeen just before the break in the Scottish League Cup Final. Jimmy Nicholl fizzes a ball to Robert Fleck on the right of the Dons' box. Fleck finds Durrant, who nods a pass down to McCoist on the edge of the 18-yard line and then back-flicks the ball to Durrant who drives through several defenders before drilling a low shot under Jim Leighton to give the Light Blues the lead.

7 December 2002

A wonderful run by Fernando Ricksen sets up Rangers' third goal of the first half against Celtic at Ibrox. Ricksen cuts in from the right and skips past three challenges before prodding the ball into the box where Shota Arveladze gets a toe to direct it towards Michael Mols, who takes a touch before poking it past Rab Douglas to make it 3-1 in a game Gers will eventually win 3-2.

10 August 2013

Rangers extend their lead over Brechin City in the Scottish League One curtain-raiser at Ibrox. There seems little threat when Nicky Law picks up the ball 25 yards from goal, but he opts to have a low shot from distance and it arrows into the bottom-left corner to put Ally McCoist's men 2-0 up at the break.

10 April 2016

Rangers double their lead in the Scottish Challenge Cup Final. The second goal against Peterhead is a stunner, too, as right-back James Tavernier volleys home his 14th goal of an impressive season from 20 yards out with a howitzer into the top-right corner to put the Light Blues well on the way to victory against the part-timers.

13 May 2018

In an absorbing and bizarre first half at Easter Road, Rangers recover from 3-0 down to make it 3-3 just before the break. Super sub Bruno Alves levels the scores with a superb 25-yard free kick as he bends a shot over the wall and into the left-hand corner of the net in what will be a memorable day for the Portuguese centre-half.

41

23 April 1949

Rangers score a second in the space of three minutes to take command of the Scottish Cup Final. Clyde's resistance had ended on 39 minutes after conceding a penalty, and the Gers then hit the woodwork straight after, but they don't have to wait much longer for the second as Willie Waddell cuts back inside the full-back on the right-hand side of the box before sending in a teasing cross that Billy Williamson thunders home with his head from close range.

4 May 1963

Rangers take a 1-0 lead in the first Old Firm Scottish Cup Final for 35 years. With just shy of 130,000 fans inside Hampden Park, Jimmy Miller plays the ball out wide to Willie Henderson whose fine cross is turned home by Ralph Brand, stealing in at the near post to score from close range.

16 January 1973

European Cup Winners' Cup holders Rangers take on European Cup winners Ajax in the European Super Cup. A crowd of 57,000 crams in to Ibrox to see the likes of Johnny Rep, Arie Haan and the great Johan Cruyff and they aren't disappointed as the Dutch auteurs turn in a masterclass of Total Football in the first leg. Rep gives Ajax a 34th-minute lead with a silky finish past Peter McCloy but the Light Blues draw level when a fine ball from Alfie Conn finds the run of Alex MacDonald and keeper Heinz Stuy can't stop his angled shot creeping in the far right post to make it 1-1. The Cruyff-inspired visitors will go on to win 3-1 on the night.

8 April 2000

Rod Wallace takes advantage of a freak bounce to all but seal the Scottish Cup semi-final against Ayr United before half-time. Wallace, who assisted the first goal, is on the shoulder of the last defender when Jorg Albertz's pass kicks up and bounces over the Ayr man's head, allowing Wallace to race clear into the box and drill a low shot across the keeper and just inside the right-hand post to make it 3-0 at Hampden Park.

6 February 2011

Having seen an early lead snuffed out by Kris Commons, Rangers go back in front against Celtic in the Scottish Cup fifth round at Ibrox. When Nikica Jelavić sends a clever reverse ball to Steven Naismith, the Rangers man skips past Fraser Forster in the Celtic box but is brought down by the Hoops' stopper. The referee points to the spot and Steven Whittaker drills a low shot into the bottom-left corner, sending the substitute keeper Łukasz Załuska to make it 2-1 in an absorbing Old Firm clash that will eventually end 2-2.

12 March 2014

Rangers skipper Lee McCulloch completes a first-half hat-trick against Airdrie at Ibrox. With McCulloch's first two goals being from the penalty spot, this is the first from open play as he bundles an effort home from just inside the box to make it 3-0 and end the scoring for the afternoon. It also ensures that the Gers – still unbeaten all season and having dropped just four points in 28 games – are crowned worthy Scottish League One champions with eight games to go as Ally McCoist's men continue their long climb back up through the divisions after being demoted to the bottom tier.

42

20 March 1897

As they say, 'details are sketchy', but what we do know is James Millar scored Rangers' opening goal of the Scottish Cup Final against Dumbarton. Little description remains of the goal, or when Dumbarton scored their only strike – but we can at least say Millar bagged the first of five for his team.

29 April 1953

Billy Simpson scores the only goal of the Scottish Cup Final replay with Aberdeen. The first match five days earlier had ended 1-1 and was watched by just a few hundred short of 130,000 at Hampden Park while the replay draws a further 113,700. The majority of them are delighted when Simpson strikes just before the break to ultimately give the Light Blues a 1-0 victory and win the trophy for the 14th time.

12 May 2021

James Tavernier, who had led the scoring charts all season, breaks his long drought by putting Rangers 1-0 up away to Livingston in the penultimate game of 2020/21. Glen Kamara and Kemar Roofe combine to put Ianis Hagi one on one with goalkeeper Max Stryjek, who brings Hagi down as he shoots. Tavernier steps up to convert the resulting penalty and move on to 19 for the campaign, two clear of Alfredo Morelos.

43

29 May 1993

A superb passing combination results in a second goal for Rangers against Aberdeen in the Scottish Cup Final. Mark Hateley starts it, playing a pass to Pieter Huistra on the corner of the Aberdeen box. The Dutchman prods the ball back to Ian Durrant who then plays it into the path of Hateley, who had moved between his team-mates and Hateley then drills a low, left-footed shot that beats Theo Snelders on his near post to make it 2-0. It is Hateley's 29th goal of the campaign and will be enough to see off the Dons, who pull one back after the break but cannot prevent the Gers completing a domestic treble.

7 April 1996

Ally McCoist puts Rangers 1-0 up in the Scottish Cup semi-final at Hampden Park. In front of a restricted crowd of just 36,333, the game looks like being goalless at the halfway point until left-back David Robertson receives the ball from Brian Laudrup outside the Celtic box, cuts inside and fires a low, right-footed shot that the Hoops' keeper can only push out into the path of McCoist who makes no mistake from a tight angle four yards out.

24 May 2008

DaMarcus Beasley doubles Rangers' lead in the 2008 Scottish Cup Final as the Gers look for a first success in the competition for five years. A corner on the left causes all kinds of confusion in the Queen of the South defenders, who never manage to properly clear the danger, and when Carlos Cuéllar's header back into the box results in Ryan McCann and Jim Thomson colliding with each other, the ball falls to Beasley who places a low shot past the keeper from ten yards out to make it 2-0.

44

30 November 1960

Rangers continue to torment a hapless Borussia Mönchengladbach side as Ralph Brand grabs his second of the game to put the Light Blues 4-0 up at Ibrox and 7-0 up on aggregate. The Oberliga side are completely overwhelmed by Rangers' inventiveness, movement and finishing with Brand's goal not even the last of the first half.

15 May 1963

David Wilson doubles Rangers' lead on the stroke of half-time in the Old Firm Scottish Cup Final replay at Hampden Park. Ralph Brand fires in an angled low shot that keeper Frank Haffey spills and Wilson is first to react, prodding the loose ball home from close range to put the Gers 2-0 up.

28 May 1979

After two 0-0 Scottish Cup Finals against Hibs, Rangers finally score just before the break to level against the Edinburgh men in the second replay. Tommy McLean surges forward unchallenged before hitting a low shot that keeper Jim McArthur can only palm out and Derek Johnstone prods home the loose ball from close range to pull the Gers back to 1-1 at Hampden Park.

25 March 1984

With the first half of the Old Firm Scottish League Cup Final looking likely to end goalless, Rangers are given the chance to take the lead. Davie Cooper holds the ball on the left of the

Celtic box before playing a smart ball in for Bobby Russell, who checks inside Murdo MacLeod and is brought down for a penalty. Ally McCoist steps up to take the spot-kick and after a long run-up sends Packie Bonner the wrong way with a shot tucked into the bottom-right corner.

28 November 1984

Iain Ferguson scores the goal that wins Rangers the Scottish League Cup Final for the 13th time. Up against Dundee United at Hampden Park, the Gers struggle to break down the Tangerines and the first half looks to be heading for a stalemate until just before the break. A neat passing move ends with the ball being played to Ferguson just inside the box and his low snap-shot whistles inside the right-hand post to make it 1-0.

2 May 1999

Amid chaotic scenes at Celtic Park, Rangers keep their cool to double the lead against their ten-man opponents. When a corner is awarded on the right, referee Hugh Dallas is struck by a missile and has to receive treatment. The referee continues and as the corner comes in, Celtic's Vidar Riseth appears to haul down Tony Vidmar and the official awards a spot-kick. In a tinderbox atmosphere, Jorg Albertz is the coolest man in Glasgow as he steps up to send the keeper the wrong way with a textbook penalty to put Rangers in sight of a first title win to be confirmed on their great rivals' own patch.

23 April 2000

Billy Dodds scores a superb goal to put the Gers on the way to the Scottish Premier League title. The Light Blues had been in pole position and well clear of the pack for several weeks, but Celtic had prolonged the wait by picking up points here and there. Away to St Johnstone, Dodds looks to seal the race for the championship as he receives a fine pass into the box from Jorg Albertz before turning and lofting a shot into the net from the narrowest of angles to make it 1-0.

17 March 2002

Claudio Caniggia is the creator as Rangers finally break down First Division Ayr United's resistance in the Scottish League Cup Final. Ayr looked set to be going in at the break with a clean sheet intact until Argentina star Caniggia wriggles past a couple of challenges before chipping a pass through to Tore André Flo, who thumps a low shot in off the post to make it 1-0.

13 December 2020

Connor Goldson restores Rangers' lead away to Dundee United with a fine header. James Tavernier's perfect delivery from a free kick means Goldson, making an early run across the six-yard box, needs only to redirect the ball into the far-left corner of the United net to make it 2-1 on the stroke of half-time with a goal that is enough to secure another three points and keep the Light Blues 14 points clear at the top of the Scottish Premiership.

45

30 November 1960

Jimmy Millar gets in on the act as he puts Rangers 5-0 up at half-time against Borussia Mönchengladbach at Ibrox. The Light Blues are ruthless against the Germans, with Millar's goal making it 8-0 on aggregate in the European Cup Winners' Cup quarter-final second leg.

29 April 1961

Rangers grab a vital goal on the stroke of half-time in the European Cup Winners' Cup semi-final second leg away to Wolverhampton Wanderers. With snow and ice making the Molineux pitch difficult to play on, the Light Blues survive the opening stages of the game thanks to some excellent goalkeeping and fine defending. With a 2-0 lead from the first leg, the Gers know an away goal will almost certainly kill the tie and it comes from Alex Scott, who makes it 1-0 at the break and 3-0 on aggregate. Needing four goals to progress, Wolves can only muster one before full time to send Rangers into the final – the first British club to make a major European final, no less.

31 March 1992

Ten-man Rangers take the lead against Celtic in the Scottish Cup semi-final at Hampden Park. Having seen David Robertson dismissed just six minutes in, it looks likely that the Gers will struggle to contain Liam Brady's side, but Stuart McCall wins possession inside the Hoops' half and as he moves forward, he slips a ball to Ally McCoist on his left and McCoist hits a first-time shot that beats the keeper and nestles in the bottom-left corner of the net. It will prove to be the only goal of the game on a rain-sodden evening in Glasgow.

9 May 1992

The Light Blues double their lead against Airdrie in the Scottish Cup Final at Hampden Park. Airdrie are masters of their own downfall when a botched clearance lands at the feet of Stuart McCall and the midfielder plays an instant pass into Ally McCoist on the left of the box. McCoist hits an angled, first-time shot across the keeper and into the bottom-right corner to make it 2-0 on the stroke of half-time. The game ends 2-1 and Rangers' 11-year wait for a Scottish Cup triumph is finally over.

29 March 2008

Kevin Thomson scores his first goal for Rangers to beat Celtic 1-0 in the Scottish Premier League clash at Ibrox. Thomson plays a clever one-two with Jean-Claude Darcheville in the Hoops' box before tucking the ball under Artur Boruc for what will be the winning goal in a crucial Old Firm match that sees the Light Blues go six points clear at the top of the table.

45+1

25 November 1999

Rangers take a 2-0 lead over Borussia Dortmund in the first leg of the UEFA Cup fourth round. Though the Gers had started the game as underdogs against the Champions League winners of 1997, a superb goal from Rod Wallace leaves the Germans clinging on at Ibrox. Giovanni van Bronckhorst sends Jorg Albertz clear down the left and as he feigns to shoot, he cleverly cuts the ball back into Wallace's path and the English winger curls a fine shot into the bottom-right corner of the Dortmund net from ten yards to send the Rangers fans wild.

20 September 2020

Rangers recover from conceding their first goal of the 2020/21 campaign, in game eight, to level in first-half added time. Hibs had become the first side to breach the Light Blues' defence with a goal on 22 minutes, but a slick one-two on the right sees Ryan Kent send a cross towards the back post where Alfredo Morelos has time to bring the ball down before rifling high into the roof of the net from close in to make it 1-1.

3 December 2020

In an explosive end to the half, a third goal in seven minutes makes it 2-2 against Standard Liège in a Europa League group stage clash at Ibrox. The Gers had twice fallen behind to the Belgians and when Kemar Roofe digs out a shot from a tight position, it strikes the arm of a Liège defender sliding in to try and block. After initially pointing for a corner as the keeper pushes the ball wide, the referee has a change of heart and instead points to the spot. James Tavernier does what he does best and makes no mistake as he tucks home the penalty.

45+2

12 August 2020

Ryan Kent grabs his second of the campaign as the Gers go 2-0 up against St Johnstone on the stroke of half-time. Borna Barišić, who opened the scoring earlier in the half, this time is the creator as the adventurous left-back whips in a low cross from the side of the box for Kent to half-volley a low drive past the keeper from 12 yards out.

Second half

46

12 March 1949

Rangers take the lead against second-tier Raith Rovers in the Scottish League Cup Final at Hampden Park. The goal comes against the run of play, with Raith much the better side in the first half, though playing with a blustery win behind them. The brilliant Willie Thornton dances past Raith defender Willie McNaught before pausing momentarily for Torry Gillick's run into the box and the Rangers striker thumps Thornton's cross past the keeper with a powerful header to make it 1-0.

3 November 1971

Colin Stein gets his second of the night just after the restart to silence the 60,000 fans at the Estádio José Alvalade against Sporting Lisbon. In a breathless European Cup Winners' Cup second round, second leg tie, Stein makes it 2-2 on the night and 5-4 on aggregate in the Light Blues' favour with his fourth goal of the two matches.

22 March 1972

Just as they had done in the previous round against Sporting Lisbon, Rangers race out of the blocks at the start of the second half and score a crucial goal. This time it is Alex MacDonald who slams one in at the far post to send the 65,000 Ibrox crowd wild and put the Gers 1-0 up against Torino in the European Cup Winners' Cup quarter-final, second leg. It puts Willie Waddell's side 1-0 up on the night and 2-1 up on aggregate – it will also be enough to send Rangers into the semi-final.

5 May 1973

Alfie Conn scores just 17 seconds into the second half of the Scottish Cup Final to put Rangers 2-1 up against Celtic. The teams had gone in level at 1-1 at the break, but the Hoops are caught napping when Rangers immediately win possession from the kick-off and Conn chases a Derek Parlane lay-off towards the Celtic box, shrugging off the challenge of Billy McNeill before sliding a low drive past the onrushing keeper to give Gers the lead.

27 August 1988

There is more than a touch of good fortune as Rangers go 3-1 up against Celtic at a sun-drenched Ibrox. A cross from the right misses everyone and finds its way to Ian Durrant, who immediately whips the ball back in and Ally McCoist's attempt to glance a header backwards is too heavy. The ball loops up towards the goal but Celtic keeper Ian Andrews misjudges the flight and cannot prevent it going over his head and into the net.

30 May 2009

Nacho Novo climbs off the bench to score what will prove to be the only goal of the 2009 Scottish Cup Final, after replacing top scorer Kris Boyd at the start of the second period with the score 0-0 against Falkirk at Hampden Park. It takes the diminutive Spaniard just 28 seconds to make an impact with a goal worthy of winning any cup final. Novo spins away after a short thrown-in from Saša Papac and allows the ball to bounce once before firing a superb looping shot from fully 30 yards that Falkirk keeper Dani Mallo has no chance of stopping. It will be enough to give Rangers a 33rd Scottish Cup win – and as of 2021, their last success in the competition – and complete a league and cup double.

3 May 2014

Dean Shiels puts Rangers in front just after half-time on the final day of the Scottish League One campaign. Though hosts Dunfermline Athletic are second in the table, they come into the game 39 points behind the champions who are looking to complete an unbeaten season. Shiels strikes as he follows up Nicky Law's shot which had been pushed out by goalkeeper Ryan Goodfellow. The game ends 1-1 and Gers finish with 33 wins and three draws from 36 games, plus 106 goals scored and just 18 conceded.

25 February 2021

Nathan Patterson takes just 17 seconds to announce his arrival after coming on as a half-time sub. Royal Antwerp had gone in at the break 1-1 with the Europa League round of 32 second leg at Ibrox finely poised at 5-4 on aggregate in the Light Blues' favour. But Patterson makes it 2-1 to the hosts as Alfredo Morelos slips him through on the right and after a couple of touches take him into the box he hits a low shot across the keeper and into the bottom-left corner.

6 March 2021

The Gers take just 30 seconds of the second half to increase their lead over St Mirren to 3-0 at Ibrox. The ever-impressive Ryan Kent crosses into the box and Ianis Hagi controls the ball before rifling past the keeper from eight yards to seal three points. And with Celtic dropping points against Dundee United the next day, the victory confirms that Rangers are champions for the 55th time and the first time in ten years.

47

5 April 1972

Rangers' happy habit of grabbing a goal just after the restart in the European Cup Winners' Cup run of 1971/72 happens for a third round in a row. They are trailing 1-0 to Bayern Munich in the semi-final, first leg in Germany but Rainer Zobel turns the ball past his own keeper to level the scores and give the Light Blues a crucial away goal to take back to Glasgow.

23 December 2020

Rangers seal a 3-0 victory just after the restart of the Scottish Premiership clash at St Johnstone to give their fans a very happy Christmas. The inventive Joe Aribo feeds Kemar Roofe, who sees his shot beaten out by Zander Clarke but only as far as Ianis Hagi, who drives an angled shot back at goal and the keeper can't prevent it from trundling over the line.

48

20 March 2005

A classic counter-attack goal gives Rangers a 4-1 lead against Motherwell in the Scottish League Cup Final. Dado Pršo cushions a long ball back to Grégory Vignal on the halfway line and his first time ball over the Well defence puts Nacho Novo clear and he makes no mistake with a clever lob to edge the Light Blues towards a 24th League Cup win.

12 August 2020

Rangers seal three points with a third goal of the evening against St Johnstone at Ibrox. A simple set piece does the trick as James Tavernier's superb delivery spots the run of Joe Aribo, who dashes towards the near post and flashes a header into the net from close range to end the scoring and complete a 3-0 win for Steven Gerrard's side.

21 February 2021

The impressive Joe Aribo gets the goal his performance deserves to put the Light Blues 3-0 up against Dundee United and on course for three more points. Aribo plays a quick one-two on the left as he drives into the United box before unleashing a thunderbolt of a left-footed shot that zips across the keeper and into the top-left corner.

49

24 May 1972

Rangers score in the European Cup Winners' Cup within a few minutes of the restart for the fourth round in a row – and this time it's in the final against Dynamo Moscow. A huge kick from Peter McCloy is misjudged by the Russian defenders and as it bounces over them, Willie Johnston ghosts in behind and with just the keeper to beat, he slots a low shot into the bottom-right corner to make it 3-0 on the night – and despite Moscow pulling two goals back, the Gers hold on to win 3-2 and secure a first major European trophy.

19 May 1999

Former Southampton and Leeds United striker Rod Wallace scores his 27th goal of the season to settle the Old Firm Scottish Cup Final at Hampden Park. As a cross comes in from the left, Celtic repel an initial attempt on goal but the ball then falls for Wallace, who places a low shot past the keeper from six yards out to make it 1-0. It will prove to be the only goal of the game.

17 March 2002

Rangers go 2-0 up against Ayr United in the Scottish League Cup Final. The First Division outfit had held firm until the 44th minute at Celtic Park but having conceded just before the break, they ship another goal just after the restart when Paul Lovering is beaten by the pace of Russell Latapy and hauls down the Trinidad and Tobago international in the box.

Barry Ferguson sends the keeper the wrong way to double the Light Blues' advantage at Celtic Park.

24 October 2010

In an Old Firm clash where something had to give, Rangers level just after the restart with a fortuitous goal. Trailing to a goal scored in first-half added time at Celtic Park, the Light Blues make it 1-1 when Steven Davis's free kick is helped on by Kyle Lafferty and Hoops defender Glenn Loovens inadvertently turns the ball into his own net with both Glasgow giants' 100 per cent Scottish Premier League record, at stake.

15 May 2011

The champagne corks are popping around the blue half of Glasgow as Rangers all but guarantee the Scottish Premier League title. With 41 minutes still to play there is work to be done but when Nikica Jelavić arrows a 20-yard free kick into the top-right corner of the Kilmarnock net, the Gers go 4-0 up at Rugby Park and are firmly on course for the three points needed to become champions yet again.

22 November 2020

Aberdeen know it is not their day when what looks like a third Rangers goal beats their keeper via a slight deflection. Ryan Kent cuts in from the left and finds Scott Arfield, who fires a shot that hits Ash Taylor and leaves Joe Lewis wrong-footed for the third time as Gers go 3-0 up.

50

18 May 1996

Fortune smiles on the Light Blues who go 2-0 up in the Scottish Cup Final against Hearts thanks to a goalkeeping howler. Brian Laudrup twists one way then the other on the right flank before sending in a low curling cross towards the near post. With no Rangers player near, it looks like a wasted opportunity but as the Jambos' Gilles Rousset squats down to gather the ball, it squirms beneath him and through his legs on its way to the back of the net. A horror moment for Rousset and a big bonus for Laudrup and Rangers.

30 January 2008

Rangers take the lead against Hearts in the Scottish League Cup semi-final at Hampden Park in controversial circumstances. After appeals for a penalty are turned down by the referee following a possible handball by Hearts' Jose Gonçalves, the ball is cleared to Chris Burke who crosses back to skipper Barry Ferguson – who also appears to handle the ball – before stroking a shot sublimely on the turn from 15 yards to make it 1-0.

5 April 2016

James Tavernier scores the goal that seals the Scottish Championship crown for Rangers and promotion back to the top flight after a four-year absence. The Light Blues' journey had been fraught with controversy, uncertainty and the occasional shock result, but as a neat build-up down the right finds Jason Holt, his low cross is met by the swashbuckling

Tavernier who sweeps past the Dumbarton keeper from close range to give Gers a 1-0 win at Ibrox.

20 August 2020

Kemar Roofe marks his full Rangers debut with a goal to put his new club 1-0 up at Ibrox. The former Leeds United striker guides a low Borna Barišić cross past the keeper to give the unbeaten Light Blues the advantage against Kilmarnock.

10 January 2021

Alfredo Morelos gets his – and Rangers' – second to put the Light Blues 2-0 up away to ten-man Aberdeen. Joe Aribo creates the chance, weaving his magic on the right before playing a low pass to Ryan Kent who delightfully flicks it into the path of Morelos, who drills a low shot into the bottom-right corner. The Gers will win 2-1 and go 22 points clear of defending champions Celtic in what is becoming a one-horse Scottish Premiership title race.

51

16 April 1932

Bob McPhail levels for Rangers in the 1932 Scottish Cup Final. In a game watched by an astonishing 112,000 at Hampden Park, Kilmarnock take the lead three minutes before the break to stun the Light Blues – but McPhail's leveller six minutes after the restart means a 1-1 draw and the teams must do it all again in a replay.

30 November 1960

Ralph Brand completes his 34-minute hat-trick and puts Rangers 6-0 up against Borussia Mönchengladbach at Ibrox in the European Cup Winners' Cup quarter-final. Brand's third goal of the evening puts the Light Blues 9-0 up on aggregate with the best part of 40 minutes still to play.

5 November 2020

Alfredo Morelos becomes Rangers' record goalscorer in European football as he bags his 22nd for the Light Blues, pipping Ally McCoist's previous best of 21. It also puts his side 3-1 up away to ten-man Benfica and seemingly on the way to a handsome win in Portugal as James Tavernier's typically swashbuckling run down the right ends with the skipper driving into the penalty area and waiting for the perfect moment to slide the ball across the six-yard box for the Colombian to tap home with the keeper stranded. Two late Benfica goals will earn a 3-3 draw to take some of the gloss off Morelos's achievement.

27 January 2021

A solitary Alfredo Morelos goal is enough to secure a 1-0 win for Rangers at Easter Road. Hibs had been dogged opposition but their backline is eventually breached when Ryan Jack finds Steven Davis, who flicks the ball on for Joe Aribo for deftly touch it on again and Morelos finishes the move with a powerful drive for his 11th goal of the season.

52

30 November 1960

Jimmy Millar makes it two goals in two minutes as Borussia Mönchengladbach capitulate in the European Cup Winners' Cup quarter-final second leg. The woeful Oberliga side now trail 10-0 on aggregate with most of the second period still to play. It is Millar's second of the game in front of more than 38,000 Ibrox fans.

October 1963

Rangers finally break down a stubborn Morton defence in the Scottish League Cup Final at Hampden Park. Watched by a colossal crowd of 105,907, the second-tier club had deserved to reach the break goalless but the Light Blues upped the ante after the restart and within seven minutes have their reward. Willie Henderson's fine burst down the right sees him drive into the box and draw keeper Alex Brown off his line – but in doing so he makes Henderson's mind up and instead of completing a fine solo goal, he squares the ball to the unmarked Jim Forrest who taps home into the unguarded net to make it 1-0.

24 October 1964

Rangers take the lead in the 1964/65 Scottish League Cup Final after a searching long ball down the right by Davie Provan catches a Celtic defender in two minds. His bizarre attempt to clear the danger results in a galloping pony-type kick that falls straight to Jimmy Millar, who plays a simple pass to his left where the prolific Jim Forrest takes a touch before drilling a low shot past Hoops keeper John Fallon to send at least half of the 91,423 Hampden Park crowd wild.

31 March 1979

Alex MacDonald levels for Rangers against Aberdeen in the Scottish League Cup Final. The Dons had taken an early second-half lead when Duncan Davidson's header squeezed under the body of keeper Peter McCloy. But the Gers are level when sub Alex Miller cuts in from the right before playing a short pass to MacDonald who fizzes a low drive from 25 yards that deflects into the bottom-left corner of the Aberdeen net to make it 1-1.

31 August 2008

Rangers go back in front at Celtic Park with Kenny Miller scoring against his former club to make it 2-1. Miller, who had made 46 appearances for the Hoops during a year's stay, meets a Charlie Adam cross on the volley at the back post, steering his angled shot into the ground and across the keeper to put the Gers in command.

1 October 2020

Rangers grab the breakthrough against Turkish giants Galatasaray in the Europa League play-off round at Ibrox. With a place in the group stages up for grabs, the Gers take the lead when James Tavernier finds Ianis Hagi, who threads a pass into the path of Scott Arfield, the midfielder making no mistake as he beats the keeper with a smart finish.

3 February 2021

Ianis Hagi scores the only goal of the game as the unbeaten Scottish Premiership leaders Rangers see off a stubborn St Johnstone 1-0 at Ibrox and maintain a 100 per cent home record in the process. The Romanian attacking midfielder receives the ball on the right flank before drifting inside past two challenges and then firing a low, left-foot shot into the bottom-right corner. A superb effort from the son of Romania legend Gheorghe Hagi.

53

21 March 2010

Kevin Thompson is shown a straight red card after a late lunge on St Mirren midfielder Steven Thompson in the Scottish League Cup Final. With the score at 0-0, the Light Blues must play the remainder of the game with just ten men.

15 May 2011

Game, set and match. Rangers go 5-0 up away to Kilmarnock and Kyle Lafferty completes his hat-trick as the Light Blues seal the Scottish Premier League crown in style. In what is Walter Smith's last game in charge, the Gers boss is able to enjoy the minutes that remain, knowing that Celtic's 4-0 win over Motherwell will count for nothing as Kai Naismith's surging run sees him lay a short pass to his right for Lafferty, who tucks the ball home for his 15th goal of the campaign.

22 November 2020

Rangers wrap up a 4-0 win over Aberdeen to remain unbeaten in the Scottish Premiership in 2020/21. The fourth goal for Steven Gerrard's men comes when Dons defender Andrew Considine fouls Leon Balogun inside the area and the referee points to the spot. James Tavernier makes no mistake as he bangs home his 13th goal of the season to remain the Gers' top scorer and ensure the Light Blues go 11 points clear at the top of the table.

54

6 October 2002

Just 60 seconds after falling 2-1 behind at Celtic Park, Rangers level to make it 2-2 in a thrilling Old Firm Scottish Premier League clash. Lorenzo Amoruso sends Neil McCann – who had come on as a sub just moments earlier – racing down the left with a fine ball behind the Celtic defence. He crosses into the middle where Ronald de Boer sneaks in between Bobo Baldé and keeper Rab Douglas to head powerfully home.

13 May 2018

Rangers go ahead for the first time against Hibs at Easter Road to lead 4-3. Having been 3-0 down after 22 minutes, it's a fantastic comeback by the Gers, who can still pip Aberdeen to second place in the Scottish Premiership, and the goal comes as Jamie Murphy slips in Jason Holt on his left and Holt makes no mistake with a deflected shot beating the home keeper.

17 October 2020

Connor Goldson grabs his second goal to secure a superb 2-0 win at Celtic Park for the Light Blues. Scott Arfield plays an excellent one-two with Alfredo Morelos before sliding an inch-perfect cross into the box where Goldson sees his initial effort blocked by Stephen Welsh, but then prods the loose ball home to secure victory and gain a vital advantage in the embryonic title race.

8 November 2020

Rangers go 5-0 up against Hamilton Academical at Ibrox. The game had been won as early as the 19th minute when the Light Blues had gone 3-0 up. The fifth comes when Ryan Kent checks in on the left before sending a fine cross towards the back stick where Jermain Defoe sees his effort strike the post and fall to Kemar Roofe, who can't miss from a couple of yards out. It is the former Leeds United and Anderlecht man's second of the afternoon.

55

17 February 1894

Hugh McCreadie puts Rangers ahead in the first Old Firm Scottish Cup Final. In front of a Hampden Park crowd of 17,000, the Gers go 1-0 up against Celtic – runaway leaders in the league at the time – in a match few expected anything other from than a Hoops victory.

20 March 1897

Tommy Hyslop scores Rangers' second goal of the Scottish Cup Final against Dumbarton. The Gers, chasing a second success in the competition, are up against a side who had already won the Scottish Cup once and been runners-up twice.

14 April 1928

Davie Meiklejohn gives Rangers the lead in the Scottish Cup Final against Celtic. Watched by a colossal crowd of 118,115, Jimmy Fleming's shot is punched away by Celtic's Jimmy McStay – despite appearing to have already crossed the line – and the referee points to the spot. Strapping centre-half Meiklejohn steps up and puts the Gers 1-0 up at Hampden Park.

23 April 1949

Eagle-eyed refereeing by R.G. Benzie as he spots a blatant push by a Clyde defender in the box and awards the Light Blues a second penalty in the Scottish Cup Final. Clyde had halved the Gers' 2-0 half-time lead shortly after the restart but George Young casually strokes the ball into the bottom-left corner to restore the two-goal advantage.

24 October 1993

Ian Durrant puts Rangers ahead in the Scottish League Cup Final against a Hibs side who led the Scottish Premier League at the time. There seems little threat as Durrant moves towards the Hibs defence, but he plays a quick one-two with Mark Hateley to race clear in the box before sending a subtle lob over keeper Jim Leighton to make it 1-0.

27 September 2011

Trailing 2-1 against Celtic in the Scottish Premier League, Rangers see a goal disallowed and another shot thump the crossbar in a bid to get on level terms at Ibrox. Finally, the equaliser comes when Steven Davis sends a deep corner into the Hoops' box and Nikica Jelavić leaps to nod down powerfully across the keeper for 2-2.

19 September 2017

Carlos Peña puts Rangers 1-0 up away to Partick Thistle in the Scottish League Cup quarter-final tie. In what is Peña's first start for Gers, he heads home Daniel Candeias's cross to finally break the deadlock at Firhill – though the hosts will level in the dying seconds to force extra time.

25 February 2021

A superb team goal and counter-attack move puts the Gers 3-1 up at Ibrox against Royal Antwerp. In a tie full of goals, Ryan Kent scores the 11th when Glen Kamara finds Ianis Hagi on the halfway line and the Romanian immediately plays it right to Morelos, who still has plenty to do. The Colombian backs himself against the Belgian left-back as he pushes the ball past him and collects it on the other side before picking out Kent's clever dart to the near post where he buries his shot to give Steven Gerrard's side clear daylight and a three-goal advantage overall in a thrilling Europa League round of 16 second leg.

21 April 2021

Scott Wright bags his first goal for Rangers and puts the Light Blues 1-0 up away to St Johnstone. The winger receives a pass from Steven Davis before curling a fine shot past the keeper. Saints will level four minutes into added time to claim a 1-1 draw but the Gers remain unbeaten.

56

5 April 1947

Jimmy Duncanson's second goal wraps up a handsome 4-0 Scottish League Cup win over Aberdeen at Hampden Park. Duncanson's strike makes it four goals in 32 minutes for the Light Blues, who declare at four on the way to a League Cup and league triumph that season.

23 October 1988

A spectacular goal from Ian Ferguson restores Rangers' lead in the Scottish League Cup Final against Aberdeen. The Dons fail to clear a long throw from close to the corner flag and the ball bounces up near the penalty spot for Ferguson to send an acrobatic howitzer past Theo Snelders to make it 2-1.

19 April 2003

Having been stunned by Motherwell's fightback, Rangers emerge for the second half of the Scottish Cup semi-final determined to get back into the game. Fernando Ricksen releases Steven Thompson – on as a half-time substitute for Shota Arveladze – to race towards goal. The former Dundee United striker then finds Michael Mols and the Dutchman fires a low shot past keeper François Dubourdeau to make it 2-2 at Hampden Park.

24 October 2010

Kenny Miller scores his customary goal against Celtic as Rangers add a second in seven minutes at Celtic Park to take a 2-1 lead. The goal is a result of keeper Fraser Forster's poor clearance that Kai Naismith is quick to intercept and he plays a lob through to Maurice Edu. Daniel Majstorović's attempt to clear the danger falls perfectly for Miller, who volleys past Fraser to give the Light Blues the lead.

6 December 2020

James Tavernier slides home his 17th goal of an already incredible season. The skipper is on fire in the box yet again as Ryan Kent's low cross from the left is slid home by Tavernier to equal his best tally for a campaign with five months of 2020/21 still to play. It puts unbeaten Rangers 2-0 up against Ross County.

57

21 April 1962

David Wilson secures a 2-0 Scottish Cup Final win over St Mirren at Hampden Park. Wilson, having helped create the opening goal, attacks down the right before cutting in and drilling a low shot home.

6 May 1978

Rangers double their lead in the 1978 Scottish Cup Final at Hampden Park. It's a cross from the right and a header that does the trick again, just as it had for Alex MacDonald's opener, as Tommy McLean, out near the right corner flag, switches to his left foot and sends a deep cross into the Aberdeen box where Derek Johnstone plants a firm header past Bobby Clarke. It proves to be the difference, with the Dons only managing to pull one back before the final whistle.

4 November 2000

Billy Dodds makes it 5-1 against St Mirren as Rangers add a well-worked fifth to the tally at Ibrox. Barry Ferguson plays a fine ball to the overlapping Lorenzo Amoruso on the left and the Italian weighs up his options before sliding a low shot into the six-yard box with the outside of his right foot and Dodds finishes with a cleverly steered drive past keeper Derek Scrimgour.

20 September 2020

A superbly worked goal puts the Gers 2-1 up away to Hibs in the Scottish Premiership. James Tavernier's attempt to cross

RANGERS: MINUTE BY MINUTE

from midway in the Hibs half is cleared but only back to the captain and this time he zips a low pass into the feet of Scott Arfield on the edge of the box. Arfield quickly lays it off to Ianis Hagi who immediately plays it back for the midfielder to take a touch then fire past the keeper from ten yards out.

2 May 2021

Rangers take a 3-1 lead against Celtic at Ibrox. Borna Barišić, heavily involved in the Light Blues' second goal, whips in a tempting cross from the left flank and Kemar Roofe times his run and leap to perfection to bury a header past the keeper and put the Scottish Premiership champions firmly in control.

12 May 2021

Ryan Kent's 13th goal of a memorable campaign doubles Rangers' lead away to Livingston. James Tavernier's clever chip finds Kent in the middle before he plays it to his right to Alfredo Morelos who returns the favour for Kent to sweep home and make it 2-0.

58

12 March 1949

Rangers double their lead against Raith Rovers in the Scottish League Cup Final at Hampden Park. The second-tier side have battled well, but the second goal of the afternoon is a setback too far with the excellent Willie Thornton again assisting a goal, this time as he guides a header down after Shaw's long punt towards the Raith box and Willie Paton makes no mistake to ensure the Light Blues secure the new knockout trophy for the second time in its three-year existence.

27 August 1988

It's party time at Ibrox as Rangers take a 4-1 lead over Celtic in an early league clash. With the sun beating down on Glasgow, the fourth goal for the Light Blues is made in England as Mark Walters teases the Celtic defence on the right before sending a sweet cross into the middle that former Grimsby Town striker Kevin Drinkell firmly plants past keeper Ian Andrews with his head to virtually seal victory before an hour of this Old Firm clash has been played.

59

26 March 1898

Alex Smith breaks the deadlock just before the hour as Rangers take a 1-0 lead over Kilmarnock in the Scottish Cup Final. In front of an estimated 14,000 Hampden Park crowd, Smith's goal knocks the stuffing out of Killie, who are appearing in their first final.

26 October 1963

The Light Blues double their lead against Morton in the Scottish League Cup Final – and again it's Jim Forrest who does the damage. Just as Forrest had been the beneficiary of some great work by the right-winger, so left-winger Craig Watson claims an assist as he plays a clever cross into Forrest who controls the ball before lashing a fierce drive past Morton keeper Alex Brown from ten yards to make it 2-0 at a packed Hampden Park.

22 May 2005

Rangers, chasing an unlikely title triumph away to Hibs at Easter Road, finally break down a stubborn home defence as Nacho Novo's shot is deflected past his own keeper to make it 1-0 for Alex McLeish's side. But with the news that Celtic – who were two points clear at the top going into the game – are leading 1-0 at Motherwell, it means that unless there is a dramatic swing at Fir Park, the Scottish Premier League title will be going to Celtic Park and not Ibrox. Later on, with Celtic's game just a minute from the end, Rangers fans resigned themselves to being runners-up. The Light

Blues' superior goal difference meant that if Motherwell did score, Rangers would go top and be champions. But the Well didn't score one – they got two in the final 60 seconds to win 2-1 and hand the title to the Gers in the most dramatic finale to a Scottish Premier League season in living memory. The celebrations at Easter Road begin on the final whistle. The day became known as 'Helicopter Sunday' after the helicopter carrying the trophy to Fir Park literally had to switch course for Easter Road.

1 October 2020

The Light Blues double their lead against Galatasaray in the Europa League play-off round at Ibrox. In a one-off tie played behind closed doors, it is their attacking full-backs who create and convert the all-important second of the night as left-back Borna Barišić sends in a cross and right-back James Tavernier towers above everyone else to head past the keeper in a game Rangers eventually see home 2-1 to qualify for the group stages.

18 February 2021

Rangers, having fallen 2-1 behind after leading through Joe Aribo's goal, finally level against Royal Antwerp. In an entertaining Europa League round of 32 first leg in Belgium, the Gers continue to knock at the door until Borna Barišić's cross from the left sees Alfredo Morelos appear to be fouled as he shapes up to head it. VAR suggests the on-field referee should take a look at the monitor and after doing just that, he points to the spot. With James Tavernier injured, Barišić steps up to mark his 100th appearance for the club with a shot that kisses the foot of the right-hand post on its way into the net to make it 2-2.

60

27 May 1961

Alex Scott gives Rangers faint hope in the second leg of the European Cup Winners' Cup Final against Fiorentina. The damage had been done in the first leg at Ibrox where the Italians had won 2-0, and they are also 1-0 up in the second leg when Scott strikes on the hour. The Light Blues needed two more goals to take the final on away goals, but despite a valiant effort, it wasn't to be and Fiorentina seal victory with a late winner to triumph 4-1 on aggregate.

23 April 2000

Billy Dodds's second goal of the game wraps up a 2-0 victory for Rangers at St Johnstone – and another Scottish Premier League title. Dodds, who had scored a stunning first-half effort, grabs another when Seb Rozental gets to the byline on the right of goal before crossing into the middle for Dodds to volley home from six yards out.

19 April 2003

Two goals in the space of four minutes turn the Scottish Cup semi-final against Motherwell back in Rangers' favour as the Light Blues recover from 2-1 down to lead 3-2. Neil McCann wins a free kick wide on the left that Fernando Ricksen centres for Lorenzo Amoruso and the Italian defender thumps a header past the keeper from close range.

15 May 2021

The ever-alert Ianis Hagi intercepts a loose pass by Aberdeen's defence and pokes the ball through to Kemar Roofe, who takes a touch to tee himself up and then drills a fine left-footed shot into the bottom-right corner from outside the box to all but ensure the Light Blues end the 2020/21 campaign unbeaten in the league.

61

20 April 1935

Having been pegged back to 1-1 in the Scottish Cup Final against Hamilton Academical, Jimmy Smith bags his second goal of the game to put the Light Blues 2-1 up. It will be the winning goal, too, as the Gers complete a league and cup double for the 1934/35 campaign.

5 May 1973

Tom Forsyth gets the easiest goal of his career – and it turns out to be the match winner in the Scottish Cup Final. A free kick from the right by Tommy McLean finds Derek Parlane, whose glancing header hits the foot of the Celtic post before rolling across goal where Forsyth has the easiest of finishes. It will prove to be the winner as the Gers claim the Scottish Cup for the 20th time.

28 May 1979

Rangers take the lead against Hibs for the first time in the Scottish Cup Final. Having endured two dour 0-0 draws at Hampden Park and then fallen behind in the second replay, Derek Johnstone grabs his second of the game to put the Light Blues 2-1 up. Bobby Russell's cross is superbly volleyed home by Johnstone, who dispatches a side-footed shot past McArthur from eight yards out.

25 March 1984

Rangers double their lead against Celtic in the Scottish League Cup Final with Ally McCoist's second goal of the game. It's route one stuff, too, as a long ball is launched forward and as Roy Aitken goes to challenge with Sandy Clarke, it is the Rangers man who manages to get a header in and flicks it to McCoist who makes no mistake with a close-range finish to make it 2-0.

26 February 2020

Ryan Kent grabs a crucial away goal to give the Gers breathing space in the Europa League round of 32 tie away to Braga. After coming back from 2-0 down to win 3-2 at Ibrox, the Light Blues continue a remarkable fightback against the Portuguese. Ianis Hagi, who missed a penalty in first-half added time, plays an excellent ball over the Braga defence to set Kent through and he makes no mistake with a composed low finish to score what will be the only goal of the game and send Steven Gerrard's men into the last 16 of the competition.

62

24 October 1964

Jim Forrest, who bagged four goals in the 1963/64 Scottish League Cup Final, threatens to do the same in the following season's event as he scores his and Rangers' second to make it 2-0 against Celtic at Hampden Park. The prolific youngster is sent clear by a piece of Jim Baxter magic and he makes no mistake as he slots the ball past John Fallon to double the Light Blues' lead. It will prove to be the decisive goal, too, with Celtic pulling one back but still losing 2-1 as the Gers record their sixth League Cup triumph. For boyhood Rangers fans Forrest – who had only just turned 20 – it is the stuff of dreams to hit a brace against Celtic and secure another trophy in the process.

26 October 1986

Rangers break the deadlock just past the hour in the Scottish League Cup Final against Celtic. In a tense Old Firm clash at Hampden Park, the opener comes when Davie Cooper's right-wing cross finds its way to the far post where Ian Durrant expertly controls the ball with his chest before skipping past his marker and drilling a low shot past Packie Bonner and into the net to make it 1-0.

27 August 1988

The Light Blues continue the demolition Glasgow derby with a fifth goal just past the hour. With Celtic rocking badly at Ibrox having conceded twice after the break to trail 4-1, Mark Walters makes it three goals in 16 second-half minutes to make it 5-1 at a raucous Ibrox. A ball is pinged towards the Celtic box but Roy Aitken makes a terrible hash of his attempt to control it and Ally McCoist steals it off him and heads towards goal. Aitken scythes the Rangers man down, but the referee allows play to continue as Walters races in to place a low shot into the bottom-left corner and seal a famous win. The Gers declare at five, with no further scoring on the day.

31 August 2008

Charlie Adam claims his second assist of the Scottish Premier League Old Firm clash at Celtic Park as he rolls a corner to the edge of the Hoops' box where Pedro Mendes unleashes a rising howitzer of a shot that flies past Artur Boruc and into the net to put Rangers 3-1 up and firmly in control in the first battle of the Glasgow giants of the campaign.

8 November 2020

Brandon Barker puts the Gers 6-0 up at Ibrox just past the hour against a beleaguered Hamilton Academical side. A fine team build-up eventually sees Jermain Defoe receive the ball on the edge of the box. He unselfishly spots sub Barker to his right, plays a short pass into his path and Barker side-foots past the keeper from ten yards out.

11 April 2021

Ryan Kent's fantastic season continues as he scores the Gers' second goal of the afternoon against Hibs. The English winger cuts in from the left, goes past one challenge, then another before firing a superb left-footed drive in off the right post from 22 yards to make it 2-0. Though the visitors will pull one back, the Light Blues win 2-1 and preserve a 100 per cent home record for the campaign.

63

26 March 1898

Rangers grab two goals in the space of five minutes to kill off Kilmarnock. Bobby Hamilton's fine shot beats goalkeeper James McAllan to make it 2-0 in the Scottish Cup Final at Hampden Park – it will also end the scoring in the match and give the Light Blues a third final success in four years.

12 May 2019

Canadian international Scott Arfield scores the goal that secures a 2-0 win over Celtic and the Gers' first back-to-back wins over the Hoops at Ibrox for seven years. Finnish playmaker Glen Kamara is the architect, turning his marker smartly to give himself space on the left before threading a ball towards Jermain Defoe. The former Spurs striker lets the ball go through his legs and into the path of Arfield, who shrugs off a challenge before sliding a low shot past the onrushing Celtic keeper Scott Bain. With a game to go, it reduces the gap at the top of the table to six points as the Gers continue to close in on their cross-city rivals.

3 December 2020

Having twice been behind in the Europa League group stage clash with Standard Liège, Rangers finally go in front with the fifth and final goal of an entertaining game at Ibrox. Ryan Kent is the provider, bursting into the box on the left before finding Scott Arfield who makes no mistake with a cool finish from 15 yards. The 3-2 victory sees the Gers into the knock-out round of 32 with a game to spare.

64

24 November 1996

Having seen a two-goal lead wiped out, Rangers go back in front against Hearts in an enthralling Scottish League Cup Final at Celtic Park. And it's a piece of Paul Gascoigne magic that does the trick as the England midfielder glides forward, drifting past one challenge before curling a low shot into the bottom-right corner to make it 3-2.

25 May 2003

With the news that Celtic are 3-0 up away to Kilmarnock, Rangers need to find more goals against Dunfermline to ensure the Scottish Premier League title heads to Ibrox and not Celtic Park on a tense last-day shoot-out between the two Glasgow giants. The Light Blues had gone 34 minutes without adding to their 3-1 first-half lead until Neil McCann is fouled on the left flank. He takes the free kick himself and whips the ball in towards the six-yard box where Ronald de Boer rises to head a magnificent goal and make it 4-1. It is the Dutchman's 20th of the season.

21 February 2021

Alfredo Morelos wraps up victory over Dundee United as he puts the Light Blues 4-0 up at Ibrox. The goal is a reward for his refusal to give up on lost causes as he chases a defender's pass back and the United keeper's attempt to clip it back to his team-mate strikes Morelos and rebounds into the empty net.

65

17 February 1894

Two goals in ten minutes stun champions-elect Celtic in the Scottish Cup Final at Hampden Park as the Glasgow giants battle it out in a major showpiece game for the first time. The Hoops are on the ropes as outside-left John Barker doubles Rangers' lead to make it 2-0 and put the Gers within sight of an historic victory.

30 November 1960

Harry Davis completes the rout of German side Borussia Mönchengladbach as he scores the Light Blues' eighth of the game. With a place in the European Cup Winners' Cup semi-final booked, the Gers declare at 8-0 and 11-0 on aggregate with no further punishment.

8 November 2020

Rangers are awarded a penalty when Jermain Defoe is bundled over in the box as Hamilton Academical's day goes from bad to worse. Defoe is fouled as he is about to pull the trigger, giving the referee an easy decision. James Tavernier blasts the spot-kick down the middle to make it 7-0 at Ibrox.

66

28 October 1990

Rangers level against Celtic in the Scottish League Cup Final. The Hoops had taken the lead earlier in the second half, with the Light Blues still furious that a first-half penalty hadn't been awarded when Packie Bonner appeared to bring down Ally McCoist in the box. The equaliser comes when a long Richard Gough pass is played up towards Mark Hateley who nods it on to McCoist on the edge of the box and as he controls it and tries to turn his man, Mark Walters runs in to hit the loose ball and fizz a low shot past Bonner from 18 yards to make it 1-1 and ultimately force extra time at Hampden Park.

7 April 1996

Brian Laudrup puts Rangers 2-0 up in the Old Firm Scottish Cup semi-final at Hampden Park. With Celtic playing a very high line, the Dane picks up the ball and can see a yawning gap behind the Hoops' defensive line so he plays a lob to the right flank before continuing his run and Gordon Durie returns the favour, looping the ball back into Laudrup's path where he chests the pass down before calmly lobbing the onrushing keeper from the edge of the box to double the Gers' lead and effectively book a final berth in the process.

18 May 1996

A wonderfully executed volley by Gordon Durie puts Rangers firmly on the way to Scottish Cup Final glory. Already leading Hearts by a couple of goals at Hampden Park, Brian Laudrup races down the left flank, looks up and sees Durie's dart into the box and sends a knee-high cross into the middle where Durie meets it sweetly with a side-foot volley that arrows the ball into the far right of the net.

24 November 1996

Paul Gascoigne scores his second goal in the space of three magical minutes with another stunning individual effort. Gazza has the ball wide on the left before jinking past one defender and heading towards goal. He spots Charlie Miller on the edge of the box and plays a low pass in before darting into the box where Miller nutmegs a Hearts defender. Gazza collects with his left foot and then steers it past the keeper with his right to make it 4-2 and effectively seal victory in the Scottish League Cup Final at Celtic Park. The Jambos will pull a late consolation goal back but the Light Blues comfortably see out the few minutes that remain.

8 April 2000

Billy Dodds gets his first of the game as Rangers go 4-0 up against Ayr United at Hampden Park in the Scottish Cup semi-final. The goal begins with an outrageous piece of showboating from Andrei Kanchelskis on the right flank. The Russian winger, with time and space, stands on the ball and then puts his hand over his brow as though looking out to sea before playing a pass to Claudio Reyna, then dashing on to Reyna's return ball and crossing in low into the six-yard box where Dodds slides home at the far post.

31 May 2003

Lorenzo Amoruso scores what will prove to be the only goal of the Scottish Cup Final against Dundee. The Italian defender profits from a set piece after Zurab Khizanishvili is punished for barging into Steve Thompson and Neil McCann's resulting free kick is glanced home from close range by the head of Amoruso after 66 minutes. With Dundee unable to respond, the Gers win 1-0 and complete a seventh domestic treble in the process to cap off a wonderful campaign for Alex McLeish's talented side.

26 April 2009

Steven Davis and Kris Boyd again combine well to double Rangers' lead in the Scottish Cup semi-final at Hampden Park. Davis, progressing towards the St Mirren box, waits until Boyd makes a perfectly timed run and slides the pass through to the striker, who calmly slots home to register his 100th goal for the club and make it 2-0.

23 January 2021

Ryan Jack starts and finishes the move that puts Rangers 4-0 up against Ross County. Jack plays the ball to Cedric Itten, who lays it off to Ianis Hagi. The Romanian then drives into the box before spotting Jack's run and his low pass is side-footed into the bottom-right corner.

67

25 October 1975

Alex MacDonald scores the only goal of the game as Rangers edge the Old Firm Scottish League Cup Final at Hampden Park. Celtic fail to deal with a cross to Derek Parlane in the box and when the striker hooks the ball into the middle, the clearance is poor and knocked back in towards the penalty spot where MacDonald meets it on the full with a powerful header to give the Light Blues a 1-0 lead they will defend until the final whistle. It is Rangers' eighth League Cup triumph.

25 May 2003

Though it's not quite party time at Ibrox, it's getting somewhere near it as Steven Thompson squeezes home Neil McCann's cross to make it 5-1 against Dunfermline Athletic. That puts the Gers in command of the final-day title shoot-out with Celtic needing to better the margin of Rangers' victory and currently only 3-0 up away to Kilmarnock. McCann wriggles past the full-back on the left and crosses towards the near post for Thompson to beat a defender and the keeper and bundle the ball over the line.

2 February 2005

Having seen a two-goal lead halved and then watched in agony as a Dundee United shot hit one post and then the other before bouncing out, the Light Blues retake control of the Scottish League Cup semi-final. Nacho Novo races down the left flank before putting a knee-high cross in towards the near post where Belgian Thomas Buffel arrives to dispatch a neat volley home from close range and make it 3-1.

24 October 2010

Kenny Miller gets another goal against Celtic to effectively wrap up a 3-1 win at Celtic Park. His second of the Scottish Premier League Old Firm clash comes from the penalty spot, when the ref decides substitute Kirk Broadfoot is fouled by Daniel Majstorović's challenge, amid protests from the home players who felt Broadfoot had dived. Miller strikes high to the keeper's left and the ball flies into the net via the post. Rangers' win ends Celtic's 100 per cent start to the season, while the Gers' flawless start to the campaign continues.

27 September 2011

Rangers go 3-2 up in an end-to-end Old Firm clash at Ibrox. The Gers, unbeaten in the Scottish Premier League, had seen an early lead become a 2-1 advantage to Celtic before levelling after the restart. The third goal comes after yet another fine cross for Gregg Wylde causes mayhem for the Celtic defence and when a loose ball drops to Kyle Lafferty, he has a couple of shots blocked before finally slotting home a low drive from close range.

20 February 2020

Trailing 2-0 to Portuguese side Braga in the Europa League round of 32 clash at Ibrox, Rangers' European adventure appears to be ending in the first leg. But Ianis Hagi has different ideas and sparks an incredible comeback for Steven Gerrard's side. Steven Davis spots Hagi in space on the right of the box and plays it across where the Romanian controls with his right, then cuts inside one challenge and zips a low left-footed shot in off the foot of the right-hand post to halve the deficit.

68

17 February 1894

John McPherson all but seals victory in the inaugural Old Firm Scottish Cup Final. The Gers make it three goals in 13 minutes against a Celtic side who had coasted to the league title when McPherson makes no mistake from close range to make it 3-0 at Hampden Park and, despite a late consolation goal for Celtic, Rangers hold out to win 3-1 and claim their first Scottish Cup triumph.

15 September 1971

Willie Johnstone grabs a priceless equaliser for Rangers in the European Cup Winners' Cup first round, first leg away to Stade Rennais. Philippe Redon had given the French side the lead after just 11 minutes but the Light Blues level midway through the second when the unmarked Johnstone fires a cross from a corner home from close range.

13 May 2018

Jason Holt's eventful day continues as he puts Rangers 5-3 up away to Hibs, who had led 3-0. Holt, with a goal and an assist already, gets his second assist when his long-range shot clips Josh Windass to wrong-foot Hibs keeper Ofir Marciano and seemingly end the hosts' hopes of pinching third in the Scottish Premiership. Holt's day, however, will take a dip as first he is sent off and then he watches on as Hibs fight back to make it 5-5 in added time. Though the point ensures the Light Blues finish third in the table, news that Aberdeen in second have lost means the last-gaps Hibs goal has prevented Champions League football for another season for the Glasgow giants.

29 October 2020

Alfredo Morelos grabs the only goal of the game as Rangers maintain a 100 per cent Europa League group stage start. Hosting Lech Poznań at Ibrox, Morelos equals Ally McCoist's European goalscoring record as he climbs off the bench to head home a Borna Barišić cross for his 21st European goal in just 36 matches.

12 September 2020

Kemar Roofe grabs his second goal as a Rangers player and puts his team 3-0 up against Dundee United at Ibrox. Scott Arfield gets the assist as he drills a low shot towards goal that Roofe gets a touch on to divert it in the opposite direction. A clever finish by the former Leeds United forward.

69

20 March 1897

John McPherson scores Rangers' third goal of the Scottish Cup Final against Dumbarton. McPherson had scored in the Gers' previous Scottish Cup triumph three years earlier and his effort at Hampden Park all but wraps up victory against the Sons.

4 May 2002

In an ill-tempered Old Firm Scottish Cup Final, Rangers come from behind to level for the second time at Hampden Park. After a free kick is awarded just outside the box and slightly right of centre, Barry Ferguson lines up the set piece before curling a shot over the wall and into the top-left corner of the net to make it 2-2 and set up a grandstand finish.

30 January 2008

Rangers double their lead against Hearts in the Scottish League Cup semi-final at Hampden Park. While there had been protests from the Jambos players and fans at Barry Ferguson's opener, there are no complaints as Jean-Claude Darcheville turns in a Chris Burke cross at the back post to make it 2-0 and book a place in the final for the Light Blues.

7 November 2019

Rangers move closer to the Europa League knockout stages with victory over Porto at Ibrox. In an electric atmosphere against the wily Portuguese, it is inevitably Alfredo Morelos who opens the scoring with a superb volley. Ryan Jack's cross into the Porto box finds Morelos, who takes a slight touch with his left foot before zipping a powerful angled shot across the keeper and into the left-hand corner of the net to put the Light Blues on track for three points.

26 November 2020

Kemar Roofe scores a superb goal to put Rangers 2-0 up against Benfica at Ibrox, just seconds after seeing his appeals for a penalty turned away by the referee. Borna Barišić and Glen Kamara combined down the left, then Barišić plays the ball to Ryan Kent who leaves it for Roofe who collects and heads towards the box before checking inside and firing a powerful shot into the top-left corner from 20 yards. But although that seems to have wrapped up victory, just as had happened three weeks earlier in Portugal, Benfica score twice late on to take a point and a creditable 2-2 Europa League draw.

8 August 2020

As easy and direct as they come as Alfredo Morelos scores to put Rangers 2-0 up against St Mirren at Ibrox. A James Tavernier corner falls right in the mixer and Morelos will never get an easier header as he directs the ball past the keeper from point blank range.

8 November 2020

The prolific James Tavernier scores his second goal in the space of five minutes as Rangers declare at eight against a poor Hamilton Academical side. It is a pity there are no fans inside Ibrox to enjoy the Scottish Premiership romp by the leaders, and even more so because of Tavernier's fantastic campaign to date as he follows up a Kemar Roofe shot by scooping a loose ball over the keeper from seven yards out to make it 8-0.

70

20 April 1932

Rangers go 2-0 up against Kilmarnock in the Scottish Cup Final replay at Hampden Park. Watched by a record midweek crowd of 105,695, the Gers are ahead from a first-half goal by Jimmy Fleming but it isn't until 20 minutes from time that the Light Blues get the second their play deserves as Fleming doubles the lead with a typically clinical finish.

15 May 1963

Ralph Brand scores his second of the Old Firm Scottish Cup Final replay. The Gers – who had been held by Celtic 12 days earlier – are much the better side in the replay and when Brand tries his luck from 25 yards out, Celtic keeper Frank Haffey makes a hash of his attempted save and the ball squirms past him to make it 3-0 and seal a 15th Scottish Cup success.

25 April 1964

After a tightly contested first 70 minutes in the Scottish Cup Final, Rangers take the lead from a simple set piece. Willie Henderson lofts a corner into the Dundee box and Jimmy Miller rises to head the ball down and into the centre of the goal to put the Gers 1-0 up and send much of the 120,982 crowd into raptures at Hampden Park.

27 April 1966

Having drawn the Scottish Cup Final 0-0 against Celtic five days before, the replay at Hampden Park is an equally tense

Old Firm affair. Although the Hoops had been marginally in the ascendency, the breakthrough finally comes when Willie Henderson's low angled shot is only partially cleared to the edge of the box where Danish full-back Kai Johansen thunders an unstoppable shot past Celtic keeper Ronnie Simpson to put the Gers 1-0 up. With no further goals on the night, it secures a 19th Scottish Cup success for the Light Blues. It is also the third time in four years that Rangers had scored a goal in the 70th minute of the showpiece match.

26 April 2009

Rangers book a place in the Scottish Cup Final with a third goal against St Mirren at Hampden Park. The Saints, by that time starting to rock, fail to clear a cross from Nacho Novo and as the ball falls to Kenny Miller, he plays a quick one-two with Steven Davis – who had been involved in the first two goals – and Miller sends a shot bobbling past the keeper to make it 3-0 and seal victory for the holders.

2 January 2021

Rangers start the new year in the best possible fashion – with a victory over Celtic at Ibrox. In what will be a fitting 50th-anniversary tribute to the 66 people who died in the Ibrox disaster, Steven Gerrard's side clinch the only goal of the game when James Tavernier's excellent cross is flicked on by Joe Aribo and on to Celtic's Callum McGregor who attempts to head it clear but it strikes his shoulder and beats his own keeper for what will be the only goal of the game. It also sends Gers 19 points clear at the top of the Scottish Premiership.

71

20 March 1897

Alex Smith scores goal number four for Rangers against Dumbarton, who are flagging against the Light Blues' superior fitness and experience. Smith's effort is the Gers' second goal in three minutes and kills off any hopes of a comeback for the Sons. Records fail to show if the score at the time was 4-0 or 4-1. What we do know is the Light Blues were in complete control.

24 May 2008

Kris Boyd drags a tiring Rangers over the line with what will prove to be the winning goal in the 2008 Scottish Cup Final against Queen of the South. In a dramatic game at Hampden Park, the Light Blues – who had seen a 2-0 lead wiped out in the space of three second-half minutes – were playing their 68th match of an exhausting campaign but have just enough gas in the tank to win the trophy for the first time in five years as Boyd rises to head DaMarcus Beasley's corner into the roof of the net from six yards out to make it 3-2 and seal victory against a spirited opponent.

21 March 2010

Rangers look to have shot themselves in the foot for the second time as Danny Wilson is shown a straight red card for pulling back St Mirren's Craig Dargo. The referee judges the foul to have denied a clear goalscoring opportunity and Wilson is dismissed just 18 minutes after team-mate Kevin Thompson had also been sent for an early bath. It leaves

Walter Smith's side 19 minutes of normal time to hang on with just nine players.

Barry Ferguson leads the celebrations as Rangers score against Celtic in the November 2000 Old Firm clash at Ibrox.

Rangers celebrate after winning the penalty shootout Scottish League Cup Final match against Dundee United at Hampden Park (16 March 2008)

James Tavernier is joined by Alfredo Morelos as the skipper celebrates scoring Rangers' second goal in the 2019 Scottish League Cup semi-final against Hearts with 47 minutes played.

Colin Stein opens the scoring against Dynamo Moscow in the 1972 European Cup Winners' Cup Final in Barcelona (May 1972)

Derek Parlane scores Rangers' first goal in the 3-2 Scottish Cup Final win over Celtic (May 1973)

Derek Johnstone is forced to jump over the ball as Davie Cooper scores in the Scottish League Cup Final against Celtic at Hampden Park (March 1978)

Ally McCoist celebrates scoring against Celtic with Davie Cooper in the Scottish League Cup Final. Rangers won the game 3-2 (March 1984).

Ally McCoist tucks home a spot-kick in the 1984 Scottish League Cup Final against Celtic (March 1984)

Paul Gascoigne celebrates his second goal for Rangers as the Light Blues seal the SPL title with a 3-0 win against Aberdeen (April 1996).

Kris Boyd celebrates his second goal against St Mirren and his 100th goal for Rangers as the Light Blues ease past St Mirren in the Scottish Cup semi-final at Hampden Park (April 2009).

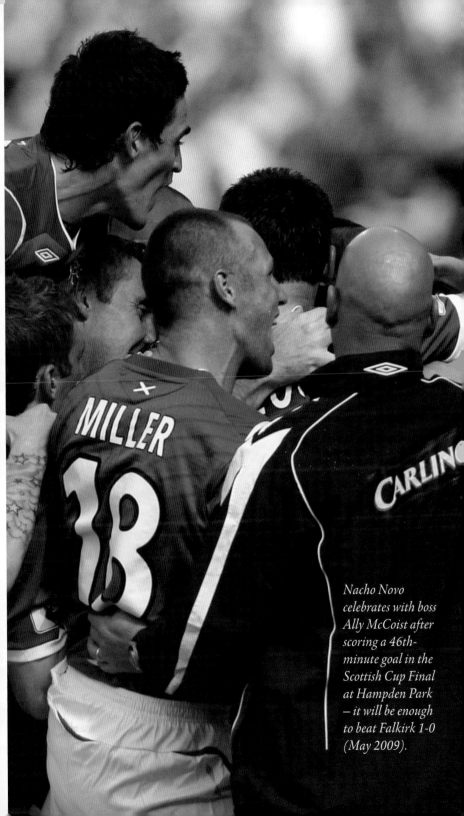

Nacho Novo celebrates with boss Ally McCoist after scoring a 46th-minute goal in the Scottish Cup Final at Hampden Park – it will be enough to beat Falkirk 1-0 (May 2009).

Ryan Kent of Rangers celebrates his goal with Joe Aribo as Rangers take a 2-0 lead against Dundee United at Ibrox in the Scottish Premiership. The Light Blues went on to win 4-1 (February 2021).

Ianis Hagi scores the only goal of the game as Rangers beat St Johnstone 1-0 at Ibrox in the Scottish Premiership (February 2021).

72

8 April 2000

Billy Dodds grabs his second goal in six minutes as Rangers go 5-0 up against Ayr United at Hampden Park in the Scottish Cup semi-final. Sebastián Rozental is the architect as he slips in slide-rule pass into Dodds's path and he takes one touch before taking it past the keeper and rolling the ball into the empty net as the First Division side start to capitulate in the closing stages.

24 March 2012

With champions-elect Celtic reduced to nine men, Rangers finally increase their lead through Andy Little. It's something of a scruffy goal – not that the majority of Ibrox gives two hoots – as a goalmouth scramble ends with Little poking home from close range to make it 2-0 and almost certainly deny Celtic winning the title. It is Little's first touch since coming on as a sub.

6 December 2020

The Light Blues seal three points away to Ross County as an own goal puts Steven Gerrard's side 3-0 up. Connor Goldson switches play to the right with a fine pass to James Tavernier, who cuts into the box and seems to have set up Alfredo Morelos but before the Colombian can score, Callum Morris slides in to put the ball into his own net.

17 January 2021

Cedric Itten rescues a point for Rangers and preserves the Light Blues' unbeaten Scottish Premiership season. They had been trailing to a first-half goal at Motherwell but the Swiss striker grabs his fourth goal in three games against Well as he heads home Borna Barišić's deep cross from the left to make it 1-1, though Gers' 14-match winning league run is finally ended.

73

19 April 2003

Rangers finally put daylight between themselves and Motherwell by going 4-2 up in the Scottish Cup semi-final. Kevin Muscat works a one-two with Fernando Ricksen and then crosses into the box where the unfortunate David Partridge nods beyond his own goalkeeper to all but end the contest at Hampden Park. Though Well later pull a consolation goal back, Rangers win 4-3 to progress to the final after a thoroughly entertaining 90 minutes of football.

7 November 2019

Two goals in the space of five breathless minutes see off Porto at a rocking Ibrox. Alfredo Morelos had opened the scoring on 69 but Steven Davis kills off the Portuguese in an absorbing Europa League group stage clash. While Morelos's goal had been delightful, the Gers' second is a tad scrappier as Davis collects the ball outside the box and drills in a low shot that deflects off a Porto defender and wrong-foots the keeper on its way into the net to make it 2-0 – a scoreline Steven Gerrard's men comfortably see out.

19 December 2020

Rangers had been behind since the sixth minute of the home clash with Motherwell before finally levelling against a determined and well-organised opponent. Inevitably, skipper James Tavernier is involved as he floats a deep cross into the box from the right flank and for once, the Well defence fails to deal with it. Ryan Kent manages not only to keep the ball alive but controls it and tees up Kemar Roofe, who thumps the ball into the roof of the net to make it 1-1 and set up a big finish.

74

20 March 1897

James Millar's second goal of the game wraps up what will be a comprehensive 5-1 Scottish Cup win over Dumbarton at Hampden Park. It is a third Gers strike in six minutes and it completes the scoring.

28 November 1981

Trailing to a Ralph Milne goal two minutes after the break, Rangers' hopes of winning the Scottish League Cup appear to be receding with barely 15 minutes remaining in the final against Dundee United at Hampden Park. But the Light Blues continue to press for an equaliser and on 74 minutes they are duly rewarded as John MacDonald is fouled chasing a long ball, resulting in a free kick on the edge of the Tangerines' box. Davie Cooper doesn't disguise his intentions as the only man over the ball and he steps up, curling a left-footed shot over the wall towards the top-right corner of the net and keeper Hamish McAlpine can only push the shot into the roof of the net to make it 1-1.

8 August 2020

Alfredo Morelos scores a second in the space of five minutes to seal a second successive win of the campaign for Steven Gerrard's men. Borna Barišić is sent clear down the left flank and though he spots Morelos, he seems to first hesitate and then crosses into the middle where a defender and the keeper contrive to miss the chance to clear and it falls to Morelos anyway. He taps home into the unguarded net from a couple of yards out, putting the Gers 3-0 up at Ibrox.

75

20 April 1932

Bob McPhail – who scored Rangers' equaliser in the first game against Kilmarnock – scores the third and final goal of the Scottish Cup Final replay. McPhail's strike makes it 3-0 in front of a huge Hampden Park crowd and is no more than the Gers deserve after a dominant display to claim a seventh Scottish Cup triumph.

5 April 1998

Rangers finally break the deadlock in a Scottish Cup semi-final played at Celtic Park – against Celtic. With Hampden Park undergoing vital renovation work, the crowd is roughly split between the two Glasgow rivals and in a tight encounter there is little between the teams. The first goal was always going to be crucial and there is no surprise when Ally McCoist is the man to score it as Jorg Albertz gallops down the left flank before sending a perfect cross into the box where McCoist needs only to slightly adjust his neck muscles to power a header past the keeper and make it 1-0.

17 March 2002

Claudio Caniggia seals a Scottish League Cup Final win over Ayr United with a superb volley to make it 3-0 at Celtic Park. The Argentinian, who created the opening goal, times his run to perfection as Neil McCann's cross comes in from the left to guide a deft volley past the keeper and into the left-hand corner of the net from close range.

6 October 2002

In a topsy-turvy Old Firm clash, Rangers go back in front at Celtic Park with Hoops keeper Rab Douglas having something of a nightmare. The Celtic keeper is at fault for a third time in the game as he spills Arthur Numan's long-range effort into the path of Shota Arveladze, who forces the ball home from close range to make it 3-2 – though Celtic will score again to earn a 3-3 draw.

20 February 2020

A wonderful individual goal by Joseph Aribo levels against Braga at Ibrox. The Portuguese had led 2-0 just eight minutes earlier until Hagi pulled one back and Aribo brings parity in the Europa League round of 32 first leg as he picks up a pass 25 yards from goal and then somehow wriggles past four or five Braga players before tucking a low shot past the keeper to make it 2-2 and spark wild celebrations.

20 September 2020

A world-class strike from Swiss striker Cedric Itten – his first goal for the club – puts the Light Blues 4-0 up away to Motherwell. Scott Arfield plays a precise pass in from the right flank to Itten, who flicks the ball up before turning and rifling a powerful shot into the top-left corner of the net.

76

2 May 1999

The goal that creates history by wrapping up a title for Rangers at Celtic Park for the first time comes 14 minutes from the final whistle with the home side reduced to ten men and crowd trouble marring the Old Firm clash throughout. Jonatan Johansson, who had replaced Gabriel Amato, plays the ball through a porous Celtic defence for Neil McCann who races clear, rounds the keeper with ease and slots into the empty net to make it 3-0 and ensure Rangers are crowned champions for the first time on their oldest rivals' home turf.

77

12 May 1981

John McDonald's second goal of the game seals a 4-1 Scottish Cup Final replay victory over Dundee United at Hampden Park for the Gers. With the Tangerines chasing a goal that would have given them some hope of a rousing finale, gaps are left at the back and when Ian Redford picks up the ball inside his own half on the left, he has all the time in the world to move forward and then play an inch-perfect pass to set McDonald in on goal and despite a poor first touch, he just gets a toe end as the keeper comes out to send the ball rolling into the net to complete a handsome win.

4 November 2000

Kenny Miller grabs his fifth – and Rangers' sixth – as the ruthless Light Blues take St Mirren apart at Ibrox. It's another fine team effort as Arthur Numan is played in on the left of the Saints' box before picking out Billy Dodds on the edge. Dodds tees up Miller who fires a thunderous drive into the top-left corner from 20 yards out to complete an unforgettable day for the 21-year-old rookie.

2 February 2005

Rangers all but seal a place in the Scottish League Cup Final by taking a 4-1 lead over Dundee United at Hampden Park. It's a set-piece goal that does the trick as Fernando Ricksen curls a shot past the wall and into the bottom-left corner.

24 March 2012

Rangers ensure there will be no Celtic title party at Ibrox as Ally McCoist's men go 3-0 up against the nine-man Hoops. In what will be the last Old Firm Scottish Premier League clash for several years ahead of the Gers' imminent demotion to the bottom tier of Scottish football, Steven Davis powers through the middle on the counter-attack before playing it to his left for Lee Wallace, who had started the move by winning the ball in his own half, and he drills a low shot under Fraser Forster to seal victory and give the Gers fans something to cheer. Celtic will pull two late goals back but the game ends 3-2 to the Light Blues.

28 November 2015

Rangers finally get the second goal their dominance deserves in the Scottish Challenge Cup semi-final at Ibrox. Just over 22,000 had braved the dreadful weather and had watched the Light Blues denied by the impressive Saints keeper Jamie Langfield on several occasions – and almost concede a shock equaliser when St Mirren struck the bar on 67 minutes. Sub Dean Shiels plays a smart pass out to Martyn Waghorn on the left of the Saints' box and his low cross is turned home by Kenny Miller to finally give the hosts some breathing space.

20 August 2020

Ryan Kent bags the goal that settles a 2-0 win over Kilmarnock at Ibrox and ensures the Light Blues remain unbeaten at the start of the 2020/21 campaign. Brandon Barker, snapped up on a free from Manchester City, scampers down the left before finding James Tavernier at the far post. After the captain sees his shot blocked, he then tees up Kent, who thumps home from just inside the box with a typically assured finish.

78

31 August 2008

An Old Firm howler by Celtic keeper Artur Boruc leads to Rangers going 4-1 up at Celtic Park. With both sides reduced to ten men after two quick red cards, it is Rangers who profit as Kirk Broadfoot's poor cross is misjudged by Boruc, who merely directs it to the feet of Kenny Miller who then rolls it past a defender on the line to seal three points in a game the Gers eventually win 4-2.

79

25 February 2021

Borna Barišić gets his third penalty against Royal Antwerp to finally kill off the lively Belgians' challenge at Ibrox. Alfredo Morelos attempts to stay on his feet after having his ankle clipped just inside the box and the referee points to the spot. Barišić, standing in for regular taker James Tavernier, emphatically strikes home from the spot having bagged two spot-kicks in the first leg. It makes it 4-2 on the night and 8-5 in the Europa League round of 32 second leg.

80

14 April 1928

Sandy Archibald makes it 4-0 in the Old Firm Scottish Cup Final at Hampden Park. The Light Blues had taken full advantage of the strong wind that had been blowing at Hampden Park with goals from Davie Meiklejohn, Bobby McPhail, and Archibald – but Celtic had failed to use the wind in the first half when it was behind their backs. Archibald thumps a shot past Hoops keeper John Thomson from 20 yards to complete the rout in front of more than 118,000 fans. The victory is Rangers' first in the Scottish Cup for 25 years.

5 April 1998

Having set Ally McCoist's opening goal up just five minutes earlier, Jorg Albertz scores the all-important second himself – and it is a worldy. The German midfielder probably never scored a better or more important goal in his Rangers career than this as he collects the ball inside his own half before driving towards the Celtic box. Albertz glides past a couple of challenges with ease before reaching the edge of the area and thundering a left-footed shot across keeper Jonathan Gould and into the top-right corner to send 22,000 Rangers fans wild at Celtic Park – the one-off 'neutral' venue for the Scottish Cup semi-final that Gers eventually win 2-1. A stunning goal and worthy of settling any game.

18 May 1996

Game, set and match as Rangers go 4-1 up in the Scottish Cup Final against Hearts. Yet again, Brian Laudrup is at the heart of the move – the Dane had scored twice and assisted another – as he wriggles free of a challenge midway inside the Hearts half before driving towards goal and finally laying it to his right where Gordon Durie takes one touch inside of a challenge before rifling a shot high into the roof of the net to seal victory at Hampden Park.

2 February 2005

Steven Thompson scores a superb half-volley to put Rangers 5-1 up against Dundee United in the semi-final of the Scottish League Cup. A flowing attack sees the ball played out to the right where Maurice Ross curls a low cross towards the penalty spot and Thompson arrives on cue to sweep a powerful volley into the bottom-left corner as the Gers finish with a flourish.

20 September 2020

Motherwell's poor defending from set pieces continues as Rangers go 5-0 up at Fir Park. James Tavernier's corner is dealt with poorly by the home defenders and the loose ball falls to Cedric Itten, who prods home from close range for his second of the game.

4 October 2020

Brandon Barker finally sees off a spirited and stubborn Ross County as Rangers continue their magnificent start to the 2020/21 season. The former Manchester City winger is sent clear by Ianis Hagi and though he is forced wide by backtracking defenders once inside the Staggies' area, he has the confidence to cut back and jink past a couple of defenders before drilling a low shot past the keeper from the centre of the box to make it 2-0 and seal another three Scottish Premiership points in the process.

7 February 2021

Brian Easton's own goal looks to have given Rangers a late 1-0 victory away to Hamilton Academical. At a freezing New Douglas Park, the Gers grab the lead as Borna Barišić's cross is driven into the six-yard box and the ball strikes Easton and flies past his own keeper. But the Accies will score with the last kick of the game to secure a well-earned 1-1 draw.

81

24 October 1993

A superb goal from super sub Ally McCoist is enough to secure yet another Scottish League Cup success for Rangers. Hibernian were good value for the 1-1 scoreline going into the closing stages, but when a long throw-in from the left of the box bounces up to McCoist, the Light Blues' striker – back to goal – sends a spectacular overhead shot into the top-left corner to make it 2-1 and give keeper Jim Leighton no chance.

10 August 2013

When Andy Little is bundled over by Brechin City's Paul McLean in the box, the referee awards a penalty and sends McLean for an early bath. It gives Rangers a chance to finally put the first Scottish League One game of the campaign to bed, with Brechin having doggedly stayed in the contest going into the final ten minutes. Ian Black steps up to take the spot-kick and though keeper Smith saves it, the ball falls directly back to Black who converts to make it 3-1.

23 January 2021

Connor Goldson scores Rangers' fifth goal against Ross County to complete a 5-0 win at Ibrox. Borna Barišić sends an outswinging corner in from the left and Goldson stoops to head the ball into the bottom-right corner to complete a comprehensive win for the Scottish Premiership leaders.

82

20 February 2020

Ianis Hagi completes a remarkable turnaround at Ibrox as he puts the Light Blues 3-2 up against Braga in the Europa League round of 32 first leg. The Gers had trailed 2-0 with two-thirds of the game gone, but goals from Hagi and Joe Aribo bring Steven Gerrard's men back from the dead and Hagi's free kick gives the Light Blues a slender advantage to take to Portugal. His effort from 20 yards takes a mighty deflection off the wall which loops up and into the opposite side of the goal it was heading for – and despite the keeper's best efforts, he can't keep it out.

19 December 2020

Rangers come from behind against Motherwell to go 2-1 up with a second goal in nine minutes. James Tavernier's corner somehow misses players from both sides before bouncing on the turf and up where Cedric Itten is lurking at the back post and reacts by heading into the roof of the net for his first Ibrox goal.

83

18 February 2021

Rangers make it 3-3 away to Royal Antwerp with a well-worked goal as the clock ticks down. Sub Ryan Kent, probing on the edge of the box, plays a one-two with Alfredo Morelos before jinking inside of a challenge and then curling a powerful shot past the keeper from 12 yards to give Steven Gerrard's men parity in the Europa League round of 32 first leg and seemingly take a draw and three away goals back to Ibrox – though the Gers weren't quite finished.

12 May 2021

Rangers ensure they will go into the final game of the season unbeaten in the league as they seal a 3-0 win at Livingston. Joe Aribo's excellent skills on the wing enable him to send Cedric Itten away and the Swiss bursts into the box before picking out Ianis Hagi's run for the Romanian youngster to slot a low shot into the bottom-left corner.

84

29 March 1961

Rangers grab a crucial second goal in the European Cup Winners' Cup semi-final, first leg at Ibrox. A 1-0 lead would have been an advantage to take to Wolverhampton Wanderers in the second leg, albeit a precarious one, so when Ralph Brand converts with what was his only chance of the game it doubles the Light Blues' advantage with the opportunity of being the first British side in a major European final edging ever closer.

26 October 1986

A controversial penalty gives Rangers a 2-1 victory and secures another Scottish League Cup success. Celtic had fought back to level the scores just 14 minutes earlier and as an enthralling Old Firm encounter seemed to be heading towards extra time, a free kick on the right is floated into the Celtic box and as Terry Butcher and Roy Aitken go for the cross, neither get there but instead collide and the referee awards a spot-kick to the Light Blues. Davie Cooper steps up to slot the ball home and secure victory.

21 March 2010

Having seen two players sent off in the second half, nine-man Rangers launch a rare counter-attack against St Mirren. Nacho Novo, Kenny Miller and Steven Naismith lead the charge, and when Naismith crosses towards the penalty spot, Miller leaps superbly and heads the ball down powerfully into the bottom-left corner to make it 1-0 and send much of Hampden Park wild and win the Scottish League Cup for the 26th time. An incredible way to win the trophy and a wonderful goal by Miller.

28 November 2015

Martyn Waghorn's 18th goal of the season wraps up victory against St Mirren in the Scottish Challenge Cup semi-final at Ibrox. The English striker collects the ball some 40 yards out and jinks his way past two defenders before drilling an angled low shot past keeper Jamie Langfield into the bottom-right corner to book a place in the final against Peterhead.

85

2 May 1999

Rod Wallace gets caught up in all the fire and brimstone at Celtic Park as he reacts angrily to a late challenge by Vidar Riseth. His raised-hand reaction results in a red card from referee Hugh Dallas – a pity with the title already sewn up and the Gers 3-0 up. It temporarily levels the teams to ten men each before Celtic have another player, Stéphane Mahé, dismissed in the time that remains. Eight other players are booked in total to make it three red cards and eight yellow cards.

18 May 1996

Gordon Durie completes a hat-trick to remember as Rangers wrap up a 5-1 win in the Scottish Cup Final against Hearts. The fifth goal also confirms a hat-trick of assists for man of the match Brian Laudrup, who races down the right before sending a superb cross towards the back post where Durie arrives on cue to power a header home and score his third goal in 19 memorable minutes.

10 November 2004

Dado Pršo scores a dramatic late equaliser in the Scottish League Cup quarter-final at Ibrox. With Celtic leading 1-0 from the 65th minute, time looks to be running out for the Light Blues until a cleverly worked move sees Hamed Namouchi's low drive pushed out by keeper David Marshall – but only into the path of a head-bandaged Pršo, who is on hand to tap the ball into the empty net and send the game into extra time.

2 February 2005

The quick-thinking Barry Ferguson is the architect for Rangers' sixth goal of the Scottish League Cup semi-final against Dundee United. The returning hero, making his second debut after re-signing from Blackburn Rovers, takes a quick free kick by lofting a chip from the halfway line into the path of Nacho Novo who races clear of the Dundee United defence and allows the ball to drop over his right shoulder before tucking home his second of the game and making it 6-1 in the process as the Gers run riot at Hampden Park.

10 August 2013

Substitute Dean Shiels puts the icing on the cake for newly promoted Rangers on the opening day of the Scottish League One campaign. The 44,000-plus Ibrox crowd are brought to their feet when Shiels receives the ball on the left corner of the Brechin City box, then cuts back inside one challenge and curls a superb shot over the keeper and into the roof of the net from 18 yards out to make it 4-1. Terrific stuff from the youngster.

10 April 2016

Any lingering hopes Peterhead had of getting back into the Scottish Challenge Cup Final are ended when Rangers are awarded a penalty five minutes from time. Jason Holt's run into the box is ended when Peterhead skipper Steven Noble pulls him down and Andy Halliday confidently converts the spot-kick to make it 3-0 at Hampden Park.

86

23 October 1988

Ally McCoist is the fox in the box as he sweeps home from close range to secure a 3-2 Scottish League Cup victory over Aberdeen. The Dons had struggled all game with set pieces and when a corner finds the head of Richard Gough, he nods it into the six-yard box where it deflects into McCoist's path and the prolific Light Blues legend makes no mistake from a couple of yards to secure a sixth League Cup triumph of the 1980s and a 16th in total since the competition began some 43 years earlier.

8 April 2000

It's a 20-minute hat-trick for Billy Dodds as Rangers continue to rout First Division outfit Ayr United. Andrei Kanchelskis is the creator again as he collects a long pass out to the right flank and kills the ball before taking on the left-back, whipping in a looping cross and finding the head of Dodds who nods the cross over the keeper and just beneath the crossbar to make it 6-0.

20 March 2005

Greek defender Sotirios Kyrgiakos puts the icing on the cake as Rangers' Scottish League Cup Final rout of Motherwell is complete. It's a stunning header, too, as when a corner comes in from the right, Kyrgiakos soars to power it on the full past the keeper and in off the right post to seal a wonderful afternoon on the tenth anniversary of legendary Rangers star Davie Cooper's untimely death.

16 March 2008

Rangers are handed a lifeline in the Scottish League Cup Final – by Dundee United's Mark Kerr. Kerr, who had been one of the best players on the pitch, receives the ball on the edge of his own box and is caught in two minds what to do. He elects to nudge it back towards his own goalkeeper but doesn't spot Kris Boyd, who nips in and slots it past Łukasz Załuska to make it 1-1 and force extra time at Hampden Park.

7 December 2013

Bilel Mohsni wraps up a 3-0 Scottish League One win over Ayr United at Ibrox as Rangers record a 20th win in succession. From a corner, Lee McCulloch sees his header saved by Ayr keeper David Hutton and Mohsni forces the ball home as Gers continue their 100 per cent start to the campaign and move 16 points clear at the top.

87

25 October 1987

Rangers grab a late equaliser against Aberdeen to force extra time in the Scottish League Cup Final at Hampden Park. In an absorbing contest that had seen the Dons lead 1-0 and Rangers fight back to lead 2-1 before the Dons re-took a 3-2 advantage, the Light Blues press for a third. When a cross is cleared to Jimmy Nicholl just inside the halfway line, he half-volleys it back to the edge of the Aberdeen box where Graham Roberts heads down towards Ian Durrant and as he controls the ball, Robert Fleck dashes in to bury a low shot to make it 3-3.

12 September 2020

Scott Arfield gets the goal his all-round performance merits as he puts the icing on the cake against Dundee United. The Canada skipper receives the ball from Ianis Hagi and he curls a fine shot past the keeper to make it 4-0 and ensure the Light Blues stay top of the Scottish Premiership on a day when Steven Gerrard's side set a new Scottish top-flight record of seven clean sheets from seven games played.

3 March 2021

Alfredo Morelos grabs a late winner to see off a determined Livingston and secure a 1-0 victory for the men from Govan. The goal comes when Glen Kamara finds Steven Davis just inside the box and Davis fires a shot that Livi keeper Stryjek pushes wide, but Morelos is on hand to drive home the loose ball for his 14th of the season. The win means Steven Gerrard's side need just four more points to win the Scottish Premiership title.

88

26 October 1963

Jim Forrest completes his hat-trick as Rangers go 4-0 up in the Scottish League Cup Final at Hampden Park. The Gers striker – who had scored twice and made another – must have thought his chance of going home with the match ball had passed, but he receives a neat pass from Craig Watson and then slots home coolly. Forrest's magical day wasn't quite over yet, however.

28 November 1981

With time running out and extra time looking likely, Rangers snatch victory and an 11th Scottish League Cup triumph in the process. Pressing for a winner, the ball finds its way to sub Ian Redford 25 yards from goal and Redford wastes no time with an audacious chip that floats just over the fingertips of Dundee United keeper Hamish McAlpine to secure a dramatic 2-1 victory at Hampden Park.

2 February 2005

Steven Thompson completes the Scottish League Cup semi-final rout over Dundee United by scoring the seventh and final goal of the night at Hampden Park. Barry Ferguson fires in a piledriver from 20 yards that the United keeper spills and it is Thompson who pokes home his second of the night to make it 7-1 and book a place in the final against Motherwell.

15 May 2021

Jermain Defoe's goal two minutes from time completes a 4-0 victory for Scottish Premiership champions Rangers, who end the campaign having not lost a single game. Defoe is fed the ball in the box and he feigns a shot to fool two defenders before tucking home a low shot with a trademark finish of a natural born goalscorer. Gers move on to 102 points as a result – the first time in the club's history that a century or more of points have been racked up and also means that with 19 straight home wins, a 100 per cent home record is completed in style.

89

26 October 1963

Jim Forrest creates history as he scores his fourth of the game to seal a 5-0 Scottish League Cup victory over Morton at Hampden Park. The 19 year-old boyhood Rangers fan – who would score 145 goals in 163 games for the club – scores his second goal in as many minutes as he fires a long-range shot that deceives keeper Alex Brown before nestling in the right-hand corner of the net to complete an incredible individual performance and secure the trophy for the Light Blues.

25 April 1964

Having seen a 1-0 lead wiped out just 45 seconds after the restart, Rangers go back in front against Dundee in a dramatic end to the 1964 Scottish Cup Final. With the match seemingly headed for a replay, Jim Baxter finds Willie Henderson on the left of the Dundee box. He cuts back inside of a challenge to get back on his favoured right foot, then chips a cross to the far post where Jim Miller rises to head the ball which loops over the keeper and two defenders into the far top-left corner to make it 2-1. It is Miller's second of the game.

8 April 2000

Sebastián Rozental finishes what he started as he grabs his second goal and Rangers' seventh in a totally one-sided Scottish Cup semi-final against Ayr United at Hampden Park. The Chilean had scored the opener on seven minutes and completes the job on a rare outing for the senior side. It's harsh on the First Division team, who had visibly wilted in the final third of the game, and as Neil McCann chases a long ball down the left he cuts into the box unchallenged before sending a low cross into the middle for Rozental to slide home.

10 April 2016

Kenny Miller wraps up a 4-0 Scottish Challenge Cup Final win with a well-deserved goal moments before the final whistle. A low cross from the right finds its way to Miller on the left of the six-yard box and he sweeps a low drive past Peterhead keeper Graeme Smith to secure a first Challenge Cup triumph for the Gers at Hampden Park.

90

25 April 1964

Rangers make it two goals in a minute to win the Scottish Cup Final against Dundee. With the Dark Blues chasing a last-gasp equaliser, Rangers win possession and move smoothly up the pitch, with Ralph Brand eventually finding David Wilson on the edge of the box and his low drive is parried by the keeper leaving Brand an empty net to make it 3-1 for the Gers and send the vast majority of Hampden Park wild.

31 March 1979

Rangers grab a last-minute winner to take the Scottish League Cup in the most dramatic fashion. With Aberdeen's defensive lynchpin Doug Rougvie sent off for violent conduct, the ten-man Dons look to have forced extra time when a free kick is awarded on the right of their box. Tommy McLean floats the ball across and Colin Jackson ghosts in to time his run and header to perfection and thump the ball past keeper Bobby Clark and win the game 2-1. It is the Light Blues' tenth Scottish League Cup triumph.

4 November 2000

Neil McCann wraps up a handsome Scottish Premier League win for the Light Blues as he makes it 7-1 with the last attack of the game. Rangers had been too good for St Mirren from the kick-off and the elegant Barry Ferguson plays a pass to Jorg Albertz halfway inside the Saints' half where the German, in turn, sees Dodds's clever run, feeds the ball into his path and Dodds slots a low shot just inside the left-hand post as the champions turn on the style at Ibrox.

17 March 2002

Claudio Caniggia wraps up a man-of-the-match display with his second goal of the afternoon to complete a 4-0 Scottish League Cup Final win over Ayr United at Celtic Park. It's something of a scruffy effort as Fernando Ricksen's cross from the right is misjudged by the Ayr keeper, who sees it slip through his hands and on to Caniggia's head, and the Argentine reacts by heading the ball goalwards from point-blank range. Despite an attempted clearance by a defender, the ball had already crossed the line. It is the first trophy won by the Light Blues under manager Alex McLeish.

4 May 2002

With the Old Firm Scottish Cup Final finely poised and heading for extra time, Neil McCann launches one final burst down the left flank. He gets level with the Celtic box before sending a curling cross into the middle where Peter Løvenkrands times his run to perfection to head the ball past the keeper and seal a dramatic 3-2 win.

11 August 2012

Andy Little saves Rangers' blushes with a 90th-minute equaliser against Peterhead to earn an opening-day 2-2 draw. The Scottish Third Division minnows looked set for a famous win as the Gers settled into life in the bottom division, but a corner headed towards goal is bundled over the line at the death by Little to secure a point for Ally McCoist's men.

18 February 2021

Borna Barišić caps his 100th appearance for Rangers by striking home his second penalty of the night to give the Light Blues a vital 4-3 victory away to Royal Antwerp in the Europa League round of 32 first leg. When Alfredo Morelos picks out Ryan Kent on the edge of the Belgians' box, Kent hits a shot towards goal that strikes a defender. There is no appeal from Kent but the referee points to the spot with Abdoulaye Seck penalised for handball – and earning a second booking in the process. Barišić steps up to thump a shot high into the top-right corner to seal a dramatic victory.

11 March 2021

There aren't many saves in *Rangers: Minute by Minute* because often they aren't recorded or highlighted in games where there are goals – but this stunning stop on 90 minutes is worthy of note. It didn't win any trophies or titles, but it earned a 1-1 draw for the Gers away to Slavia Prague as Allan McGregor dived down to his left to prevent a towering header from Lukáš Masopust from giving the Czech side a last-gasp win in the Europa League round of 16 first leg. It was a stunning save from McGregor, who showed that at 39 he'd lost none of his agility.

6 December 2020

Jermain Defoe puts Rangers 4-0 up away to Ross County. Cedric Itten is the provider, hassling the Ross County right-back before relieving him of the ball and crossing to Defoe in the six-yard box. With his back to goal, Defoe spins around and drills home a low shot to complete a fine victory in the Highlands and put Steven Gerrard's men 14 points clear at the top of the Scottish Premiership.

Added Time

90+1

28 November 2015

St Mirren's miserable trip to Ibrox is completed by an added-time own goal as Rangers complete a 4-0 Scottish Challenge Cup semi-final victory in style. Sub Dean Shiels bursts into the box on the left before crossing low into the six-yard box where Sean Kelly slides the ball past his own keeper as the Light Blues book a place in the final against Peterhead.

90+2

25 May 2003

With tension from the Ibrox stands filtering down, the unbearably knife-edge scenario of Rangers and Celtic being level on goal difference going into added time continues. With Rangers 5-1 up against Dunfermline Athletic and Celtic winning 4-0 away to Kilmarnock, where Alan Thompson has also missed a penalty, it means that the Gers are winning the title on more goals scored as things stand. However, a Celtic goal in the dying seconds at Rugby Park would mean Martin O'Neill's side would be champions instead. What the Light Blues needed was an insurance policy and when Neil McCann is felled in the box in added time, they have the chance to get it. Mikel Arteta steps up and sends the keeper the wrong way, meaning that Celtic would have needed to score twice more to deny Alex McLeish's men. Moments later Ibrox erupts as news filters in that it is all over at Kilmarnock and Rangers are champions by a single goal on goal difference to end what had been one of the most thrilling title races of all time.

22 October 2020

Kemar Roofe's goal of the season contender wraps up a 2-0 Europa League group stage win away to Standard Liège. The hosts, who had trailed since the 19th minute, had hit the woodwork twice and threatened to at least take a point until Roofe's outrageous effort. The former Leeds United and Anderlecht striker picks up the ball in his own half and knocks it past Nicolas Gavory before unleashing a shot from the halfway line – officially recorded at 54.6 yards – that gives

Liège keeper Arnaud Bodart no chance. It is later confirmed to be the longest shot ever scored in the Europa League. It took power, swerve, height, vision and incredible self-belief to even attempt such an effort but it turned into arguably one of the most spectacular Rangers goals of all time.

25 February 2021

A second penalty of the night and a fourth conceded overall by Royal Antwerp puts a nice sheen on the scoreline at Ibrox. Opoku Ampomah clambers over sub Scott Wright as he cuts into the box on the right and the referee awards the Light Blues another chance to score from 12 yards. Borna Barišić hands duties over to another sub – Cedric Itten – who blasts home to make it 5-2 on the night and 9-5 overall in what had been a ridiculously entertaining two legs between the clubs. It also means Steven Gerrard's men have progressed into the Europa League round of 16 for the second successive season.

2 May 2021

Jermain Defoe rolls back the years as he puts Rangers 4-1 up at Ibrox against Celtic. The Hoops, already deposed from their Scottish Premiership title, back off as Defoe runs towards the box and the former England striker defies his 37 years of age as he twists one way and then another, putting Stephen Welsh on his backside before rolling a low shot past the keeper and into the bottom-right corner of the net to complete a handsome victory for the Gers.

90+3

28 February 2010

Rangers snatch victory in the last minute of added time to take a giant step towards a second successive Scottish Premier League title. The Light Blues went into the game seven points clear of Celtic but need a win to increase that to a hefty ten-point lead. It looks as though the ten-man Hoops might hang on for a 0-0 draw when one last attack sees a shot from the edge of the box blocked. Kris Boyd then has an effort scrambled out, but Maurice Edu forces the ball home from a yard or so out to send Ibrox wild and put the Gers firmly in control of the championship race.

27 September 2011

Steven Naismith ensures Ally McCoist's first Old Firm clash as Rangers manager ends in victory with a smart volley in added time. The Light Blues had led 3-2, but when Steven Davis manages to fire a cross in from the left, Naismith has plenty of time and space to guide a shot past Fraser Forster to make it 4-2, claiming his second goal of the game and sealing three points in the process.

90+4

19 December 2020

Kemar Roofe finally ends Motherwell's dogged resistance with the goal that seals three points. Steven Gerrard's side had trailed 1-0 until the 73rd minute, but recovered to lead going into added time and Roofe's second of the game makes it 3-1 as Joe Aribo jinks into the box on the left before trying to tee up Cedric Itten. A defender blocks that pass but Aribo then pokes it back off his toes to Roofe, who thumps a powerful shot into the top-right corner.

Extra Time

94

19 September 2017

Daniel Candeias restores Rangers' lead four minutes into extra time away to Partick Thistle as he cuts in from the right before lashing a low shot home to put the Light Blues 2-1 up at Firhill and place one foot in the Scottish League Cup semi-final.

96

17 April 2016

Barrie McKay scores a stunning long-range goal as Rangers go back in front against Celtic in extra time. With a place in the Scottish Cup Final at stake, the Gers – in the wilderness since being demoted to the bottom tier – go 2-1 up when the ball is worked forward towards the Hoops' box and McKay is on hand to thump a howitzer of a shot into the top corner and send one half of Hampden Park crazy.

97

3 October 2002

Substitute Neil McCann puts Rangers 3-0 up in extra time against Viktoria Žižkov in the UEFA Cup first round, second leg. After losing the first leg 2-0 to the Czech side, Ronald de Boer grabs two goals to level the aggregate scores and sends the match into an additional 30 minutes. Mikel Arteta sends de Boer clear down the right flank and his cross is dispatched by McCann to put the Light Blues ahead on aggregate 3-2. A goal from the visitors three minutes later, however, will ultimately knock the Gers out on the away goals rule.

98

20 March 2011

Nikica Jelavić scores what will be the extra-time winner against Celtic in the Scottish League Cup Final. The goal is the result of quick thinking from Slovakian winger Vladimír Weiss who takes a quick free kick on the halfway line, playing a pass into Jelavić's path and the Croatian, darting between two defenders, manages to roll a shot past Fraser Forster and sees the ball hit the right post, spin out but then back in and just goes inside the opposite upright to give the Light Blues a 2-1 win and 27th League Cup triumph.

99

19 September 2017

A superb Eduardo Herrera goal finally ends Partick Thistle's resistance in the Scottish League Cup quarter-final at Firhill. Having conceded in added time to the hosts, the Gers quickly restore their grip on the game with a Daniel Candeias effort and Herrera adds another four minutes later as a fine move sees a cross from the left go across goal without being converted – but as Candeias drills it back towards the six-yard box, Herrera expertly back-flicks past the keeper to make it 3-1.

100

3 November 1971

Drama at the Estádio José Alvalade in Lisbon as Rangers make it 3-3 in extra time against Sporting. In a thrilling tie, the hosts had matched Rangers' first-leg lead of 3-2, forcing an extra 30 minutes. In the first leg at Ibrox, Colin Stein had scored the first two goals and Willie Henderson the third – and that's what happens again in Portugal, with Henderson's strike making it 3-3 and giving the Gers a 6-5 advantage in the European Cup Winners' Cup second round, second leg. Sporting will score again five minutes before the end of extra time to make it 6-6 overall. Incredibly, the referee then orders a penalty shoot-out, which the Portuguese side wins – not realising that Rangers had won the tie on away goals. Despite the penalties fiasco, UEFA later confirms that Rangers were through to the third round.

10 November 2004

Substitute Shota Arveladze scores the winning goal to send Rangers into the Scottish League Cup semi-final at Celtic's expense. A superb, flowing counter-attack instigated by Fernando Ricksen sees the Dutch right-back break from deep inside his own half before finding Arveladze in space on the right of the Hoops' box and the Georgian squeezes an angled shot past David Marshall's near post to give the Light Blues a 2-1 victory in a pulsating tie at Ibrox.

5 August 2014

Nicky Law puts the Light Blues 2-1 up at Ibrox as the Challenge Cup tie with Hibs goes to extra time. The Gers had led through Lewis Macleod's first-half goal but the visitors levelled after the break as well as seeing a men sent off. Law curls home what will be the winner as Macleod's cross is missed by Kris Boyd and Lee Wallace.

102

12 April 2008

Nacho Novo levels from the spot in the Scottish Cup semi-final against St Johnstone. The Saints had gone ahead three minutes into extra time after the first 90 ended 0-0, but the Light Blues are handed a lifeline when referee Dougie McDonald points to the spot for Kevin Rutkiewicz's foul on Daniel Cousin, and Novo steps up to hammer the ball low past Alan Main to make it 1-1 and eventually force a tense penalty shoot-out.

103

20 April 2008

Rangers' hopes of a quadruple are salvaged in extra time against St Johnstone at Hampden Park. The Saints had gone ahead on 94 minutes after the two sides played out a tense 0-0 during normal time in the Scottish League Cup semi-final. But when full-back Gary Irvine pulls down Daniel Cousin in the box, the referee points to the spot. Nacho Novo steps up to tuck the ball into the bottom-left corner to make it 1-1 and ultimately send the game to a penalty shoot-out.

104

25 March 1984

Ally McCoist completes a fantastic hat-trick against Celtic to win Rangers a 12th Scottish League Cup triumph. The Hoops had fought back from 2-0 down to take the Old Firm final at Hampden Park into extra time but it is McCoist who settles it with his 19th goal of the season. McCoist had been fouled by Roy Aitken in the box then stepped up to take his second penalty of the game. This time keeper Packie Bonner guesses right and saves the spot-kick but only pushes the ball back to McCoist, who tucks the rebound home for the winning goal for Jock Wallace's side in front of a crowd of more than 67,000.

28 October 1990

Richard Gough shows the deft touch of a seasoned finisher to clinch the Scottish League Cup Final against Celtic. The Light Blues had come from behind to force extra time, and when a long, angled pass is played into the Hoops' box, Gough follows the flight of the ball over an attempted flick on by a team-mate and ghosts behind a defender to gently guide a shot past Packie Bonner to make it 2-1 and secure a 17th League Cup success.

109

31 May 1967

Having watched Celtic lift the European Cup a few days earlier, the chance to ensure Glasgow was the football capital of Europe was the carrot for Scott Symon's side. Playing in the Städtisches Stadion in Nuremberg and up against a Bayern Munich side that included the likes of Sepp Maier, Franz Beckenbauer and Gerd Müller, Rangers battle hard in front of a partisan German crowd of almost 70,000. Roger Hynd sees a goal disallowed in normal time and extra time is played. But it won't be Rangers' evening as a deep ball is played into the Light Blues' box and midfielder Franz Roth controls the pass then lifts the ball over Norrie Martin for what would prove to be the only goal of the game.

28 May 1979

Rangers get the goal that decides the 1979 Scottish Cup Final second replay. Played in front of a disappointing 30,602 Hampden Park crowd, the match had ebbed and flowed with Hibs taking the lead before two Derek Johnstone goals made it 2-1 to the Gers. Then Ally McLeod levelled for Hibs to send the game into extra time. With the two teams seemingly inseparable – particularly after a 103rd-minute Rangers penalty was saved – the Light Blues go 3-2 up when Davie Cooper's cross is headed past keeper Jim McArthur by Hibs defender Arthur Duncan.

110

1 May 2008

Rangers' hopes of reaching a fourth major European final take a blow in the second half of extra time against Fiorentina. With the first leg of the UEFA Cup semi-final at Ibrox ending 0-0, the sides are again deadlocked in the return in Italy, playing out another goalless 90 minutes. But when Rangers sub Daniel Cousin is accused of headbutting Fabio Liverani, he receives a second yellow card and is sent off. The Light Blues must survive the last ten minutes with just ten men in order to force penalties and they do exactly that.

113

16 March 2008

Super sub Kris Boyd rescues Rangers again in the Scottish League Cup as Dundee United fail to deal with a cross from the left and then a dinked ball in from the right as Boyd out-muscles two United defenders at the far post to nod home his second goal of the game, making it 2-2 and forcing a penalty shoot-out.

114

25 October 1992

Rangers get the goal that settles the 1992 Scottish League Cup Final at Hampden Park. John Brown moves down the left flank before sending a cross into the Aberdeen box intended for Mark Hateley, but in an attempt to prevent the Gers striker from connecting, Aberdeen left-back Gary Smith launches himself at the ball and gets just enough of a touch to send it past his own keeper and inside the right-hand post to make it 2-1. It completes a miserable match for Smith, who had also been at fault for the first Rangers goal.

118

18 March 1978

Late drama and controversy as Rangers grab a last-gasp extra-time winner to seal a 2-1 victory over Celtic in the Scottish League Cup Final at Hampden Park. Celtic appeal long and passionately that the goal shouldn't stand as Alex Miller's cross is dropped by keeper Peter Latchford and Gordon Smith is left with the simple task of knocking the ball into the unguarded net to send half of the 60,000-plus crowd wild. Latchford is convinced Alex MacDonald had impeded him but the referee says the goal stands to secure the Light Blues' ninth League Cup win.

Penalty shoot-outs

Not all matches can be decided in normal time or extra time – for those that can't, and when a result on the day is needed, it is the dreaded penalty shoot-out. Cover your eyes if you daren't look, but it might make it difficult to read what happened in this selection of Light Blues shoot-outs.

25 October 1987

After a thrilling 90 minutes and then a further half-hour of extra time, Rangers and Aberdeen are forced into a shoot-out at Hampden Park to decide the Scottish League Cup Final.

- Ally McCoist (Rangers) scores – 1-0
- Jim Bett (Aberdeen) scores – 1-1
- Davie Cooper (Rangers) scores – 2-1
- Peter Nicholas (Aberdeen) misses – 2-1
- Robert Fleck (Rangers) scores – 3-1
- Peter Weir (Aberdeen) scores – 3-2
- Trevor Francis (Rangers) scores – 4-2
- John Hewitt (Aberdeen) scores – 4-3
- Ian Durrant (Rangers) scores – 5-3

Rangers win 5-3 on penalties

6 December 2001

After a 0-0 draw with Paris Saint-Germain at Ibrox in the UEFA Cup third round and then a 0-0 second leg at the Parc des Princes, Ronald de Boer misses a penalty for the Gers in extra time, meaning a shoot-out is needed to settle the tie.

- Lorenzo Amoruso (Rangers) scores – 1-0
- Jay-Jay Okocha (Paris Saint-Germain) misses 1-0
- Russell Latapy (Rangers) scores – 2-0
- Ronaldinho (Paris Saint-Germain) scores – 2-1
- Bert Konterman (Rangers) misses – 2-1
- Mikel Arteta (Paris Saint-Germain) scores – 2-2
- Claudio Caniggia (Rangers) misses – 2-2
- Gabriel Heinze (Paris Saint-Germain) misses – 2-2
- Arthur Numan (Rangers) scores – 3-2
- Bernard Mendy (Paris Saint-Germain) scores – 3-3
- Barry Ferguson (Rangers) scores – 4-3
- Mauricio Pochettino (Paris Saint-Germain) misses – 4-3

Rangers win 4-3 on penalties

6 March 2008

Having twice come from behind late on to force a 2-2 draw – once in normal time and once in extra time – Rangers are somewhat relieved to have the opportunity to beat Dundee United on penalty kicks and end almost three years without winning a trophy.

- Willo Flood (Dundee United) scores – 1-0
- Jean-Claude Darcheville (Rangers) misses – 1-0
- Craig Conway (Dundee United) misses – 1-0
- Steven Whittaker (Rangers) scores – 1-1
- Mark de Vries (Dundee United) scores – 2-1
- Steven Davis (Rangers) scores – 2-2
- David Robertson (Dundee United) misses – 2-2
- Lee McCulloch (Rangers) misses – 2-2
- Lee Wilkie (Dundee United) misses – 2-2
- Kris Boyd (Rangers) scores – 3-2

Rangers win 3-2 on penalties

12 April 2008

After coming from behind to secure a 1-1 draw against St Johnstone in the Scottish Cup semi-final, Rangers have to battle the Saints in a penalty shoot-out for the right to take on Queen of the South in the final.

- Paul Sheerin (St Johnstone) scores – 1-0
- Steven Davis (Rangers) scores – 1-1
- Liam Craig (St Johnstone) scores – 2-1
- Steven Whittaker (Rangers) scores – 2-2
- Steven Milne (St Johnstone) misses – 2-2
- Nacho Novo (Rangers) scores – 2-3
- Andrew Jackson (St Johnstone) scores – 3-3
- Brahim Hemdani (Rangers) misses – 3-3
- Jody Morris (St Johnstone) misses – 3-3
- Daniel Cousin (Rangers) scores – 3-4

Rangers win 4-3 on penalties

1 May 2008

After 210 minutes of football without a goal in the UEFA Cup semi-final against Fiorentina, ten-man Rangers are forced into a penalty shoot-out to decide who goes into the final to play Zenit Saint Petersburg at Manchester City's Etihad Stadium (then called the City of Manchester Stadium). It's also a chance to avenge the 1961 European Cup Winners' Cup Final defeat by the Italians.

- Barry Ferguson (Rangers) misses – 0-0
- Zdravko Kuzmanović (Fiorentina) scores – 0-1
- Steven Whittaker (Rangers) scores – 1-1
- Riccardo Montolivo (Fiorentina) scores 1-2
- Saša Papac (Rangers) scores – 2-2
- Fabio Liverani (Fiorentina) misses – 2-2
- Brahim Hemdani (Rangers) scores – 3-2
- Christian Vieri (Fiorentina) misses – 3-2
- Nacho Novo (Rangers) scores – 4-2

Rangers win 4-2 on penalties

17 April 2016

After a classic Old Firm battle that fairly fizzed and crackled throughout, the Scottish Cup semi-final at Hampden Park ends 2-2 to mean only one thing – the dreaded penalty shoot-out. Which side of Glasgow would have bragging rights the next day?

- Andy Halliday (Rangers) scores – 1-0
- Charlie Mulgrew (Celtic) scores – 1-1
- James Tavernier (Rangers) misses – 1-1
- Callum McGregor (Celtic) misses – 1-1
- Barrie McKay (Rangers) scores – 2-1
- Nir Bitton (Celtic) scores – 2-2
- Nicky Clark (Rangers) misses – 2-2
- Scott Brown (Celtic) misses – 2-2
- Lee Wallace (Rangers) scores – 3-2
- Leigh Griffiths (Celtic) scores 3-3
- Gedion Zelalem (Rangers) scores – 4-3
- Mikael Lustig (Celtic) scores – 4-4
- Nicky Law (Rangers) scores – 5-4
- Tomas Rogic (Celtic) misses – 5-4

Rangers win 5-4 on penalties